International Business - New Insights on Changing Scenarios

Edited by Muhammad Mohiuddin, Slimane Ed-Dafali, Elahe Hosseini and Samim Al-Azad

Published in London, United Kingdom

International Business - New Insights on Changing Scenarios
http://dx.doi.org/10.5772/intechopen.105385
Edited by Muhammad Mohiuddin, Slimane Ed-Dafali, Elahe Hosseini and Samim Al-Azad

Contributors
Abdeslam Hassani, Hussam Al Halbussi, Paul Nwanna, Syazwan Syah Zulkifly, John Burgess, Elni Jeini Usoh, Linda Lambey, Robert Lambey, Noluthando Shirley Matsiliza, Ana Espada, Kambidima Wotela, Clive Sithole

First published in London, United Kingdom, 2024 by IntechOpen
IntechOpen is the global imprint of INTECHOPEN LIMITED, registered in England and Wales, registration number: 11086078, 5 Princes Gate Court, London, SW7 2QJ, United Kingdom
Printed in Croatia

British Library Cataloguing-in-Publication Data
A catalogue record for this book is available from the British Library

Additional hard and PDF copies can be obtained from orders@intechopen.com

International Business - New Insights on Changing Scenarios
Edited by Muhammad Mohiuddin, Slimane Ed-Dafali, Elahe Hosseini and Samim Al-Azad
p. cm.

This title is part of the Business, Management and Economics Book Series, Volume 15
Topic: Business and Management
Series Editor: Taufiq Choudhry
Topic Editors: Vito Bobek and Tatjana Horvat

Print ISBN 978-1-80356-140-0
Online ISBN 978-1-80356-141-7
eBook (PDF) ISBN 978-1-80356-142-4
ISSN 2753-894X

For EU product safety concerns:
IN TECH d.o.o., Prolaz Marije Krucifikse Kozulić 3, 51000 Rijeka, Croatia,
info@intechopen.com or visit our website at intechopen.com.

IntechOpen Book Series

Business, Management and Economics

Volume 15

Aims and Scope of the Series

This series will provide a comprehensive overview of recent research trends in business and management, economics, and marketing. Topics will include asset liability management, financial consequences of the financial crisis and covid-19, financial accounting, mergers and acquisitions, management accounting, SMEs, financial markets, corporate finance and governance, managerial technology and innovation, resource management and sustainable development, social entrepreneurship, corporate responsibility, ethics and accountability, microeconomics, labour economics, macroeconomics, public economics, financial economics, econometrics, direct marketing, creative marketing, internet marketing, market planning and forecasting, brand management, market segmentation and targeting and other topics under business and management. This book series will focus on various aspects of business and management whose in-depth understanding is critical for business and company management to function effectively during this uncertain time of financial crisis, Covid-19 pandemic, and military activity in Europe.

Meet the Series Editor

Prof. Choudhry holds a BSc degree in Economics from the University of Iowa, as well as a Masters and Ph.D. in Applied Economics from Clemson University, USA. In January 2006, he became a Professor of Finance at the University of Southampton Business School. He was previously a Professor of Finance at the University of Bradford Management School. He has over 80 articles published in international finance and economics journals. His research interests and specialties include financial econometrics, financial economics, international economics and finance, housing markets, financial markets, among others.

Meet the Volume Editors

Dr. Muhammad Mohiuddin is an Associate Professor of International Business at Laval University, Canada. He has taught at Thompson Rivers University, Canada; University of Paris-Est, France; Osnabruck University of Applied Science, Germany; Shanghai Institute of Technology and Tianjin University of Technology, China. He has published research in *Research Policy*, *Applied Economics*, *Review of Economic Philosophy*, *Strategic Change*, *International Journal of Logistics Research and Applications*, *Sustainability*, *Journal of Environmental Management*, *Journal of Global Information Management*, *Journal of Cleaner Production*, *M@N@GEMENT*, and more. He is currently the director of the Research and Study Group on Contemporary Asia (GERAC) at Laval University. He is the also co-managing editor of *Transnational Corporations Review*.

Dr. Slimane Ed-Dafali is an Associate Professor of Management (HDR) at the National School of Commerce and Management (ENCG), Chouaib Doukkali University, Morocco, where he conducts teaching and research activities. His current research is focused on entrepreneurial finance, innovation, knowledge management strategy, family business, and corporate governance. He has contributed to different research projects with various scholars and universities. He has conducted applied research studies for institutional associations like the Moroccan Private Equity Association (AMIC). He is also a member of the International Academic Association of Governance (AAIG) and the Family Business Center. Dr. Ed-Dafali also serves as a referee for several international journals.

Elahe Hosseini received a Ph.D. in Organizational Behavior and Human Resource Management from Yazd University, Iran, where she is a lecturer. She is also a lecturer at Shiraz University, Iran. Her research interests include employee voice, human resource management, and social and entrepreneurship activities to encourage entrepreneurship in developing countries. She has several publications in international journals to her credit and has participated in several conferences. Dr. Hosseini serves as an editor and editorial board member for journals such as the *Iranian Journal of Management Studies* and *International Journal of Management and Enterprise Development*. She is also a reviewer for journals such as *Sustainability*, *Transnational Corporations Review*, and *SAGE Open*, among others.

Dr. Samim Al-Azad has recently completed his post-doctoral research from Stephen A. Jarislowsky Chair in International Business at Laval University, QC, Canada". He is also an Assistant Professor of Management Information Systems (MIS), at North South University, Bangladesh. His current research interests include artificial intelligence (AI), offshore IT outsourcing, IT adoption, and Industry 4.0. His research has been published in peer-reviewed journals including the *Journal of Global Information Management*, *International Journal of Logistics Research and Applications*, *Knowledge and Process Management*, and *Con-*

temporary Management Research. He has presented several papers at international conferences, including the Academy of International Business (AIB), Pacific Asia Conference on Information Systems (PACIS), and Administrative Science Association of Canada (ASAC). He was awarded the best paper award twice for his papers at the t ASAC-2014 (IB) and ASAC-2015 (TIM) conferences. He also has experience working with BRAC (the world's largest development organization based in Bangladesh) on several projects funded by the World Health Organization (WHO) and the United Nations Development Programme (UNDP).

Contents

Preface

This edited volume is a collection of reviewed and relevant research chapters concerning developments in international business. It includes scholarly contributions by various authors and is edited by a group of experts in business, management, and economics.

The book consists of the following chapters:

Chapter 1: "A Conceptual Framework for Researching Disruptive Innovation and Innovative Business Models"

Chapter 2: "Business Intelligence: An Important Tool to Develop Dynamic Capabilities and Sustainable Innovation in the Digital Age"

Chapter 3: "Circular Systems Design: Seeking Outgrowth Based on Disruption"

Chapter 4: "Corporate Governance in the South African Public Agencies: Implications for Oversight and Accountability Mechanisms"

Chapter 5: "Perceptions of and Reactions to the HR Implementation Process in Nigeria"

Chapter 6: "Challenges and Opportunities to Internationalize the Indonesian Higher Education Sector"

Chapter 7: "Work-Related Safety and Health Issues among Food and Parcel Delivery Riders"

IntechOpen

Chapter 1

A Conceptual Framework for Researching Disruptive Innovation and Innovative Business Models

Clive Sithole and Kambidima Wotela

Abstract

The number of entrepreneurs in South Africa and, therefore, the Total Entrepreneurial Activity is lower than expected. The absence of entrepreneurial orientation is not the problem but, rather, instead of focusing on the innovative products and services, we should focus on innovative business models that change the processes. This chapter conceptualises an appropriate conceptual framework for effectively researching disruptive innovation and innovative business models at subnational level. We employ systems thinking to interrogate literature to realise three objectives. First, to understand the root causes and consequences of low innovation in new business ventures in South Africa and more specifically Gauteng Province. Second, to uncover the knowledge gap on this subject generally and specifically Gauteng Province. Lastly, to establish the most appropriate framework in innovation and entrepreneurship studies for interpreting anticipated empirical results. Eventually, this research will detail innovativeness in new business ventures after interrogating the theoretical material and empirical data and information on disruptive innovation and innovative business models. We have sufficient theoretical grounding on this subject but not empirical grounding to support some of our assertions. Even though most of the interrogations are general, it is within the context of Gauteng Province and, therefore, we may not generalise our conclusions and proposals. We do not address how innovativeness influences policies in general and we do not restrict ourselves to any specific sector.

Keywords: 4th industrial revolution, business models, disruptive innovation, innovative business models, research problem analysis, research knowledge gap analysis, theoretical frameworks, conceptual framework

1. Introduction

Crossan and Apaydin [1] describe innovation as production, adoption, assimilation and exploitation of value-added novelty in economic and social spheres. It is also the renewal and enlargement of products, services and markets as well as development of new methods of production and establishment of new systems. This makes innovation a process and an outcome. Further, innovation can be an original creation or a creation that is adopted or adapted from elsewhere. Successful business ventures are usually those that innovate. This is why established paradigms always relate innovation to entrepreneurship because the two concepts work interchangeably [2–4]. Therefore, one cannot study one without the other.

The number of entrepreneurs in South Africa, and, therefore, the Total Entrepreneurial Activity, is lower than expected. Such as status quo affects its economic growth and therefore, employment. The absence of entrepreneurial orientation is not the problem but, rather, the lack of focus on appropriate interventions. Rather, we argue that the entrepreneurship problem in South Africa even amongst the youth is due to low innovation. The failure to focus on disruptive innovation pitches the country against the leaders in innovation, therefore, making it less competitive. Further, instead of focusing on innovative products and services, we should focus on innovative business models that seek to change the way we do business.

Eventually, the aim of this research is to detail innovativeness in new business ventures after theoretical and empirical data and information on disruptive innovation and innovative business models. However, this paper is restricted to articulating the theoretical fundamentals to conceptualise 'how' the empirical part of this research may be pursued. The conceptual framework that we derive in this paper allows us to effectively research disruptive innovation and innovative business models at the subnational level. We, therefore, employed systems thinking (Section 2) to interrogate the literature for purposes of pursing three objectives: first, to understand the root causes and consequences of low innovation in new business ventures in South Africa and more specifically Gauteng Province; second, to uncover the knowledge gap on this subject—that is, what has not been done—in general in South Africa and specifically Gauteng Province and lastly, to establish the most appropriate framework in innovation and entrepreneurship studies for interpreting anticipated empirical results on disruptive innovation and innovation models.

The literature interrogation, in Sections 3 and 4, confirms that despite being the economic hub of the continent, the fifth-most populous country in Africa and the third-largest in the Southern African Development Community (SADC) region, South Africa has the lowest number of entrepreneurs in Africa, exhibiting a low Total Entrepreneurial Activity. Second, as evident in Section 5, most past and current research have focused on the person and not the context or the environment. Further, even then we are not completely aware of the problems faced by those involved in innovation in Africa or its sub-regions. Furthermore, we are not certain of the relationship between innovation and entrepreneurship sufficiently enough to decode an effective, sustainable and efficient innovative business model. The literature shows that whilst other countries, especially Spain, have interrogated the link between innovation and entrepreneurship in new business ventures [3], there is minimal research on this subject in South Africa.

Lastly, for purposes of proposing a framework for interpreting empirical results (Section 6), we situate such research within the innovation discourse. Whilst innovation has several attributes and variables, the literature suggests that we restrict ourselves to two sets: Crossan and Apaydin's [1] framework of organisational innovation and Booyen's [5] factors to interrogate abilities to pursue disruptive innovation. Further, the literature points to employing the upper echelon theory, the resource-based view, dynamic capabilities and the process theory to interpret our research findings. To this list, we add the model linking innovation and entrepreneurship because it incorporates all the frameworks mentioned above on one platform.

Arising from the literature we have interrogated in Sections 3 through 6, which we sum up in Section 7, we propose that the empirical part of this research should pursue two research questions. First, what factors can enhance disruptive innovation in Gauteng Province? This should be explicitly on disruptive innovation and not innovation in general or incremental. Second, how can we innovate business models of small and medium entrepreneurs in Gauteng Province? This should explore the ways of commercialising disruptive innovation products or services beyond the conventional ways of doing business. Therefore, other than speculating on the potential of innovation within South African new business ventures, the conceptual framework this paper provides should guide an empirical research that identifies factors underlining low innovation and entrepreneurship in South Africa. With this in mind, a qualitative research strategy and a case study design should be more appropriate. This is because our focus is not the extent of the problem but rather to detail the reasons underlying the problem. We should focus on South African-owned formal (not informal) small to medium enterprises that have been running for less than 10 years and not notable South African corporate companies. Whilst we now have sufficient theoretical grounding on this subject, we do not have, at this moment, empirical grounding to support some of our assertions. Even though most of the interrogation is general, we undertook it in the context of Gauteng Province, and therefore, we may not generalise our conclusions and proposals. We do not address how innovativeness influences policies in general, and we do not restrict ourselves to any specific sector.

This is certainly an important research trajectory for three reasons. First, whilst the link between innovation and entrepreneurship seems logical and several empirical studies – for example, [2, 4] as well as [3] – are affirmative about the link, we are yet to establish how innovation (or lack of it) leads to success (or failure) of a new business venture in different contexts. Second, empirical comparative data show that South Africa's level of innovativeness and, therefore, entrepreneurialism continues to lag behind [6], but we are yet to explain why. Relatedly, why are South African entrepreneurs notably necessity-driven and opportunity-driven rather than improvement-driven? Lastly, the research will contribute to the body of knowledge on this subject in general and more specifically to the development of entrepreneurship modules in business schools. The private or business sector has realised that entrepreneurial skills provide for business creation and self-employment, making entrepreneurship modules a key contribution in business school. Relatedly, this research might provide for decision-making information for start-up and entrepreneurship incubators that provide support to small businesses and entrepreneurs. Similarly, government departments such as the Department of Small Business Development as well as government agencies such as the Small Enterprise Development Agency (SEDA) might enhance policy formulation and implementation to improve innovation and entrepreneurship in South Africa. It may also help the Industrial Development Corporation when they assess funding applications.

2. The approach

Levy and Ellis [7] in [8] describe a conceptual framework as a proposed literature-based and literature-justified approach to the research that one intends to pursue. Therefore, as [9] has argued, it is a proposed advanced strategic plan of how empirical research (data or information collection, collation, processing and analysis) will be implemented with key decisions arising from interrogating key literature on the subject. This paper applies Wotela's [8] six-step approach to propose a conceptual framework that should guide empirical studies on disruptive innovation and innovative business models. The six steps can be grouped into three sets of activities, namely, interrogating the literature on the research problem, the research knowledge gap, and the interpretive (theoretical or otherwise) framework [8]. Therefore, these form the section headings of this paper.

3. The physical research setting; gauteng province in context

Figure 1 shows the current official boundary of South Africa and its nine provinces. The focus for this paper is Gauteng Province located towards the north-eastern side of South Africa. According to [10], it is the smallest province—covering only about 18,200 km^2, that is, about 1.5 per cent of South Africa's land cover. However, almost 25 per cent of the South African population (13.5 million) lives in Gauteng Province. About 75 per cent of this population is Black and 20 per cent is White, whilst the remaining (5 per cent) proportion is shared amongst Asians and Coloureds, with the latter slightly more than the former. Of importance to our

Source: Htonl

Figure 1.
The map of South Africa showing its neighbouring countries and its provinces (map of South Africa with English labels" by Htonl-own work. Licenced under CC BY-SA 3.0 via commons - https://commons.wikimedia.org/wiki/File:Map_of_South_Africa_with_English_labels.svg#/media/File:Map_of_South_Africa_with_English_labels.svg).

research is that Gauteng province is not only South Africa's wealthiest province but also Africa's economic hub – contributing about 40 per cent to the country's gross domestic product [11].

Formal education has been on the increase since 1994 and had reached 30 per cent in 2008 and is currently over 40 per cent. Despite the odds, science, engineering and technology are popular subjects in the province [12]. The economic activities of Gauteng Province have all the prerequisites of making it a knowledge-based economy [11, 13, 14]. Similarly, it is proposed in the Gauteng Employment Growth and Development Strategy (GEGDS) 2009–2014 that innovation should be one of the drivers of employment through small and medium entrepreneurship [15, 16]. This is possible because Gauteng spends about half of the national budget on research and development in the country [11]. One key intervention in the innovation space is the Gauteng Science Park Incubation Programme detailed in [16].

4. Low innovation in new business ventures in South Africa

The Global Entrepreneur Monitor [6] reports that sub-Saharan Africa has the lowest number of entrepreneurs on the continent. Further, compared with other sub-Saharan African countries, South Africa has the lowest number of entrepreneurs and a lower Total Entrepreneurial Activity even though its discontinuance rate – that is, the frequency at which those who attempt opt out of the entrepreneur process – is modest. Few of these entrepreneurs turn out to be successful in their business ventures. Of interest to this research is the proportion of South African youths with entrepreneurial capability standing at 25 per cent compared with an average of 60 per cent for sub-Saharan countries.

One root cause of low innovation and hence entrepreneurship is early-stage entrepreneurial activity. **Table 1** shows the motivation index and other relative parameters for early-stage entrepreneurial activity in economies participating in the Global Entrepreneurial Monitor. First of all, early-stage entrepreneurial activity in South Africa (7 per cent) is way below the African average (26 per cent). Another parameter below the African average is the improvement-driven opportunity at 35.5 per cent for South Africa compared to about 47 per cent for the continent average. This implies 35.5 per cent of South Africans in the Total Entrepreneur Activity are motivated by improvement-driven opportunities and not because they could not find work, as well as seeking to be independent or to increase their income rather than maintaining their current income.

As implied in [17], another root cause of low innovation and hence entrepreneurship is that South Africans would rather emulate 'tried-and-tested' ideas instead of creating something new. Obviously, emulating means you are competing with the best, and therefore, the business is set up to fail. Emulating or adopting ideas is not uncommon. In Spain, the proportion of firms generating new inventions is only 7 per cent, compared with 54 per cent emulating, though a notable proportion (39 per cent) does both [18].

Underlining all this, according to Booyens [5], is a lack of policy support. There are notable talented innovators in South Africa, but legislation and interventions to nurture and support them are misaligned if not just ineffective. For example, according to [19], the current labour legislation hinders innovation as well as small and medium entrepreneurship because of its human resources processes. Then there is the collision course between various interventions and legislature. The National Development

Country/ region	Early-stage entrepreneurial activity (TEA)	Necessity-driven	Opportunity-driven	Improvement-driven opportunity	Motivational index
	% of adult population	% of TEA	% of TEA	% of TEA	
Average Africa (unweighted)	26.0	26.3	71.0	46.9	1.8
Angola	21.5	24.5	72.1	43.4	1.8
Botswana	32.8	30.3	67.2	54.7	1.8
Burkina Faso	21.7	22.3	75.3	52.8	2.4
Cameron	37.4	33.5	59.2	40.5	1.2
South Africa	7.0	28.2	71.3	35.5	1.3
Uganda	35.5	18.9	80.8	54.3	2.9

Source: The Global Entrepreneur Monitor (2013). Note: Total Early-Stage Entrepreneurial Activity (TEA) refers to the total population that is about to start a business or those who have been running businesses for not more than 3 years.

Table 1.
Motivation for early-stage entrepreneurial activity in the global entrepreneurial monitor economies in 2012, by region and country.

Plan seeks to increase job opportunities by 2030, and yet SMEs shed 1.3 million jobs in 2013. Underlying this undesirable status quo are unsupportive labour laws, a weak national innovation system, a weak entrepreneurial culture, and an inability to compete with large companies that Booyens [5] raised earlier on.

5. Knowledge gap analysis: methods, data, findings and conclusions of studies on and evaluation of innovativeness in new business ventures

There are several studies worldwide on this subject in general and specifically on innovation and entrepreneur start-up rates, innovation as a strategy and how it affects performance, as well as implementation of innovation. Here we only review a selection of such studies to familiarise ourselves with what has been done so that we uncover the knowledge gap, that is, what has not been done, on this subject in general and specifically Gauteng Province. Apart from findings and conclusions, we also look out for research procedures and methods that such studies applied so that we establish some methodological options that we also can employ when undertaking the empirical part of this research.

Scholars have attempted to link innovation and firm performance. For example, [20] sought to explore and establish Tanzanian new business venture innovative activities and how this determined performance in manufacturing sector. They tracked five innovation indicators—that is, knowledge and technological information, knowledge and skills, growth performance, characteristics and capabilities and external relationships and nature of the market—over three years. Despite low levels of competition and a lack of government support or help from academic institutions, results show that new business ventures do innovate. Most support comes from fellow entrepreneurs as well as customers—this certainly needs further exploration. Further, a large number of new business ventures tend to improve on products and services initially supplied by other firms if such products or services are in demand. Therefore, one can use a firm's innovation capability to determine its performance [21]. A study by Zott and Amit [22] found a similar result, that is, an innovative business model contributes to a firm's success.

Kropp, Fredric and Shoham's study [23] examines the interrelationships amongst entrepreneurial learning, market orientations and international entrepreneurial business venture (IEBV) performance using a sample of 396 entrepreneurs. The results show that innovativeness determines the performance of IEBVs. In addition, the results show that IEBVs that include innovative concepts in their strategies perform better than those without. Purcarea and colleagues [24] got the same results in their study on 161 Romanian Small and Medium Enterprises (SMEs) that explored SMEs' approach to learning and innovation. Their findings show that SMEs' innovation depends on their business models and strategic direction. As a result, they recommend on-going interventions that promote innovation in every industry.

Studies on the implementation of innovation in new business ventures present a wide range of results and findings, therefore, presenting an opportunity to explore this subject further. Obviously, one question to pursue is why such studies have such a diverse set of results and findings. Could it be the different contexts, or are there other attributes at play? For example, [25], whose sample comprised entrepreneurs, policy makers and academics, sought to demonstrate whether Italian entrepreneurs are drivers of radical innovation. Their research shows that the views of the entrepreneurs on this subject are different from official views. The former feel like policies that support innovation are absent contrary to views held by politicians and senior technocrats. Such findings remind us of the importance of stakeholder engagement and alignment when crafting public policies.

Robson, Haugh and Obeng [26] collected data from 496 entrepreneurs in Ghana to study innovation in new business ventures. The results confirm that Ghanaian entrepreneurs are indeed innovating their products and services. Further, their results show that the level of education has an impact on the level of innovativeness. Another obvious factor is that larger firms tend to have an advantage because they have more resources to innovate.

Anokhin and Wincent's study [27] used data collected in 35 countries from 1996 to 2002 to establish the relationship between innovation and start-up rates. Similar to earlier studies – for example, [28] as well as [29] – their results show that there is no collinearity between innovation and new business start-up rates. However, they argue that this is because the relationship between innovation and entrepreneurship depends on the country's stage of development. Therefore, measuring the relationship between innovation and entrepreneurship is not as direct. Further, the results and findings cannot be generalised because the propensity of innovation differs. Entrepreneurs in less developed countries pursue necessity-based innovation that hardly advances the innovation trajectory, whilst entrepreneurs in developed countries pursue high-end innovation. Earlier, [30] had cautioned against generalising the relationship between innovation and entrepreneurship because of added complexities presented when industries and geographical locations are different.

Using a sample of 4000 enterprises including notable corporates, the South African National Innovation Survey [31] reported that about 65 per cent undertook innovative activities. Of these, about 4 per cent reported that their innovations were not only new to the South African market but also new to the world. However, caution must be exercised when reading into these figures because the sample includes well-established corporates.

Autio and colleagues [32] use Global Entrepreneurial Monitor to explore the importance of context in innovation and entrepreneurship. They demonstrate that entrepreneurial innovation seems high, and therefore, self-employment rates in developing countries are also high. Whilst self-employment rates are lower in the developed countries, the aggregated contributions of entrepreneurs to innovation is very high. Therefore, different contexts—such as technological and industry context, organisational and social contexts, institutional and policy contexts—are interdependent and influence innovation and entrepreneurship. Indeed, small and medium enterprises do exploit new technologies to start businesses using social networks as a marketing and information dissemination platform.

In sum, there are notable detailed innovation and new venture business studies on the African continent including South Africa. For an important topic, there is minimal research focusing on the South African context with the exception of [5, 33] as well as [31]. Further, most studies have explored the relationship between innovation and entrepreneurship in new business ventures in one firm or industry. Therefore, there is a lack of cross-industry or cross-sector information on the subject. In addition, most studies have not incorporated some important factors such as determinants of innovation as well as innovation challenges faced by entrepreneurs on the continent.

Other than these knowledge gaps, there are useful frameworks as well as research procedures and methods that the empirical part of this research can benefit from. For example, [26] have interrogated innovation and entrepreneurship after understanding the Ghanaian context. Examining small businesses and entrepreneurship from a historical perspective and how it has informed the current state of innovation in Ghana provides for a detailed understanding of innovation and new business ventures. This is the light in which we should interrogate the South African experience. The question is, 'what are we going to do about it?'

6. Established frameworks for interpreting empirical results in innovation and entrepreneurship studies

In this section, we explore and propose a framework that we can use to interpret anticipated empirical results in innovation and entrepreneurship studies. To do this, we need to identify and discuss innovation and entrepreneurship and the key components. Thereafter, we use our understanding of innovation and entrepreneurship and the key components to interrogate the literature on determinants and dimensions of innovation and the established frameworks that we can potentially use to interpret research findings. In sum, we explicitly link innovation and entrepreneurship to its key attributes and variables and, consequently, propose an interpretive framework.

6.1 An introduction to innovation

Several authors such as [1, 25, 34, 35] describe innovation as formulating and implementing creative ideas at the industry level, company level or business unit level. Innovation is employed to develop a product, improve a process, commercialise a product or service and solve a problem. Therefore, we can differentiate between (i.) administrative versus technical innovation, (ii.) process versus product innovation and (iii.) incremental versus radical innovation. We detail the last grouping because that is the focus of this research.

Incremental innovation implies improving on an existing product, service, process, technology, equipment, material, tool or portfolio, whilst radical innovation involves creating a product, service, process, technology, equipment, material, tool or portfolio that previously did not exist [30, 36]. There is great interest into the speed at which organisations enter into the technological space [37], leading to a wide range of nomenclature. This includes Freeman's [38] well-known typologies or strategies, namely: offensive, dependent, traditional, opportunistic, imitative and defensive as well as proactive versus reactive and follower versus leader. The others are prospectors, defenders, analysers and reactors [39]; entrepreneurial versus conservative innovators [40] and proactive versus reactive innovators [41].

The question obviously is, 'what is useful for the South African context?' We think it is the entrepreneurship aspect in innovation because of its business connotation. This implies some detail on the business model innovation that provides for improving the structure, competitive advantage, value proposition and ability to link suppliers and customers [42]. Therefore, rather than introducing a product or service, a business model as an innovation implies introducing new processes to become or remain market leaders. As stated earlier, a study by Zott and Amit [22] suggests that an innovative business model—efficiency, lock-in complementarities and novelty—contributes to a firm's success. A business model qualifies as innovation if and only if it provides substantial economic value such as creating additional demand or enlarging the customer base [43].

Shirky [44] has, however, argued that successful new business ventures tend to be those without a perfect business model and, therefore, are flexible, enabling entrepreneurs to adjust and change when the situation allows. Earlier, Andries and Debackere [45] had suggested that formulation and adjustment of business models should be in line with a firm's evolution and lifecycle. Therefore, formulation and fine-tuning business models should be an ongoing process so that the models meet the changing needs of markets. Teece [46] refers to such an approach to business modelling as push and pull. This approach allows entrepreneurs to project future scenarios and, therefore, anticipate possible problems way before they occur [47]. In sum, business models are key to innovation and entrepreneurship because, as George and Bock [48] have argued, they '...represent a unique opportunity to unlock the entrepreneurial process, evaluate the firm configuration effects, and describe and forecast the entrepreneurial outcomes' *p*461. Any good innovative idea should be supported by an innovative and suitable business model.

Two more concepts that are important are open innovation and disruptive innovation. Chesbrough [49] defines open innovation as the ability of an organisation to use'... knowledge to accelerate internal innovation, and expand the markets for external use of innovation, respectively' *p*2. This implies explicit use of internal and external systems and technologies to create value and enhance competitive advantage. Implementing open innovation provides for increased profitability [50]. However, as Bianchi and colleagues [51] have argued, implementing open innovation in small and medium-sized enterprises is a challenge because of limited financial resources and a lack of specialised knowledge. Therefore, Hossain [52] has recommended a policy that should assist small and medium-sized enterprises to adapt and implement open innovation.

We now turn to disruptive innovation, another important term that several authors have interrogated, and therefore, as Markides [43] argues, it is a debatable terminology. The literature is clear that entrepreneurs have a choice to either establish a business based on a new idea or emulate what other businesses are doing. The former is disruptive because a new idea or technology can cause new waves or change habits in the market. Therefore, disruptive innovation is a new product, service, process, technology, equipment, material, tool or portfolio that emerges and threatens to replace the existing one [53]. Alternatively, it can be a successful product, service, process, technology, equipment, material, tool or portfolio that allows an organisation to change competitive rules or create new trends [54]. Disruptive innovation has two main features. First, it provides simplicity, affordability and an unexpected replacement of the status quo. Second, disruptive innovation is an ongoing gradual process and takes time to eventually change the way things are done, customer mind-sets and consumer preferences [55].

Thormond, Herzerg and Lettice [53] have suggested a four-stage disruptive or radical innovation cycle, that is, opportunity recognition (generating and refining ideas), opportunity development (creating credible business cases), solution development (selecting compelling business cases and formulation long-term action plans) and exploitation. The last stage involves selecting marketing channels, distribution methods and investment decisions. Further, [53] point out that disruptive innovation might be an effective starting point for new business ventures. However, like open innovation, lack of funding might stifle adequate research on the idea. Other barriers include insufficient knowledge on the industry, reliance on customer perceptions and inability to challenge the innovation status quo. In sum, innovations arise from different circumstances and result in varying competitive advantages. Therefore, one has to exercise caution and not just group them into one category or under the same description.

6.2 Determinants and dimensions of innovation

Some factors, attributes, variables or determinants—internal or external within a given context—can increase an entity's capability to innovate, whilst others inhibit innovation. **Figure 2** presents Crossan and Apaydin's [1] framework of organisational innovation. More broadly, the figure has innovation classified into (i.) leadership as well as institutional and organisational arrangements for innovation, (ii.) innovation as a process, and (iii.) innovation as an outcome. Further, note that leadership as well as institutional and organisational arrangements for innovation provide for determinants of innovation—grouped at the individual and group level, organisational level and process level—whilst innovation as a process and innovation as an outcome provide for dimensions of innovation. The determinants of innovation include frameworks—upper echelon theory, resource-based view, dynamic capabilities and process theory—that one can use to interpret empirical results emanating from an innovation and entrepreneurial study.

Several authors have discussed the determinants of innovation including those presented in Crossan and Apaydin [1]. For example, Tipping and Zefran [56] as well as Hossain [52] argue that using an explicit innovative strategy, the mission, goals and strategy of new business ventures should be aligned to their absorptive and desorptive capacities. Absorptive capacity implies the ability to sense, apply and utilise newly acquired knowledge, whilst desorptive capacity implies being able to use external knowledge to one's advantage [57]. Such integration embeds innovation in the day-to-day activities of an organisation.

Earlier, Hausman [58] has argued that the close relationship between entrepreneurs and their customers in small businesses allows for quick reaction to customer needs and market demands. However, this does not give them an upper hand because

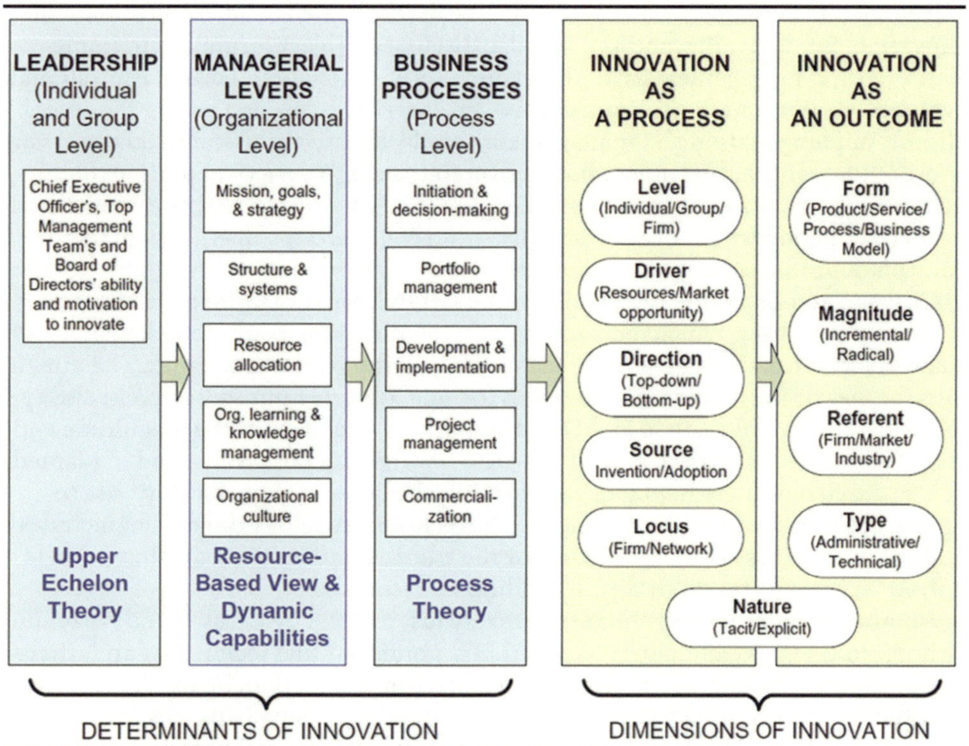

Source: Crossan and Apaydin's (2010)

Figure 2.
Crossan and Apaydin's [1] framework of organisational innovation.

they still lag behind in product innovation and technology adoption [59] probably because they also need human and financial resources and market influence to innovate more effectively [59, 60]. However, as Rosenbusch, Brinckmann and Bausch [60] have also argued, excessive resource allocation to an innovation idea without the capability to turn the idea into a viable offering can affect venture performance negatively. Therefore, apart from developing an innovative product or service, a new business venture should take a holistic strategic approach towards innovation orientation – including business modelling [61]. This will lead to an effective allocation of resources, creation of ambitious goals and nurturing of a long-term sustainable innovation culture.

Further, Rosenbusch, Brinckmann and Bausch [60] have argued that innovation orientation adopted by the entrepreneur and a focus on innovation outputs influence innovation. New business ventures with a strong approach towards innovation orientation are able to transform ideas into innovative offerings. Further, Croissan and Apaydin [1] state that knowledge management provides documenting generation of ideas and innovation systems for future reference. The leadership of an organisation can use cultural arrangements to create an enabling environment and encourage taking risks and trying new ideas.

Also, Cooper and colleagues [62] have discussed portfolio management with particular focus on the return on investment and risk. They argue that effective strategic management of resources through careful selection of projects to pursue as well as foresee what the organisation should look like in the future is a key determinant of innovation. Similarly, Bessant [63] has also discussed project formulation, implementation and management as key determinants of innovation. Formulation should involve modifying or adjusting an idea as well as trying it out first before the actual roll-out. Implementation and management should effectively attend to transforming inputs or ideas into actual innovation deliverables using a variety of tools including problem-solving cycles. Adams and colleagues [64] have discussed commercialisation and marketing to turn innovation activities into commercial value. Though important, this determinant is usually outsourced.

Croissan and Apaydin [1] provide for the self-evident dimensions for measuring innovation processes, which include level, driver, direction, source and locus as well as nature, which is also a dimension for measuring innovation outcomes. The dimensions for measuring innovation outcomes include form, magnitude, referent and type. According to Gopalakrishnan and Damanpour [34], the focus of the magnitude and referent dimensions is the degree of newness or originality of an idea and if adapted, then 'is the change incremental or radical?' It is the latter change that gave rise to the 'disruptive innovation' terminology. The technical typology dimension includes product and process specification, whilst the administrative typology dimension is centred on organisational structure and human resources.

Another important determinant, probably just implied by Crossan and Apaydin [1] if not missing, is technology. Ndabeni [33] points out that technology and, therefore, consumer preference and demand are changing faster than before. Therefore, to sustain new business ventures and remain competitive, small and medium entrepreneurs should adapt their business approaches to embrace technology [65]. For this reason, Ndabeni [33] has argued that only if they can embrace technology, South African small and medium entrepreneurs can generate employment and increase economic endogenous growth – that is, growth in the long run driven by technological factors and knowledge [66].

Much more contextualised, Booyens [5] has proposed six determinants or rather factors that enhance innovation in a firm – that is, (i.) educated or skilled labour workforce; (ii.) creativity, personal attributes and entrepreneurship; (iii.) investment in research and development; (iv.) knowledge systems; (v.) knowledge networks as well as (vi.) public support to private innovation. Obviously, *an educated or skilled labour workforce* is an essential ingredient in innovation efforts because of its potential to generate and improve upon knowledge [5, 67, 68]. Without a doubt, *creativity, personal attributes and entrepreneurship* provide for innovation [5]. This explains the heightened focus on how psychological foundations, skills and knowledge influence innovation [69]. Further, Schumpeter's 1940 theory of business cycles and development is categorical on the role of entrepreneurship in innovation [5, 70].

Booyens [5] states that *investment in research and development* is the backbone of innovation and provides for detailed exploration of solutions to key societal problems. Unfortunately, there is little or ineffective innovation in the South African manufacturing sector largely because of minimal financial and human resource investment in research and development [68]. According to Wolf [71], *knowledge systems* include creating an 'appropriate incentives regime to correct market and institutional failures in capturing technological knowledge and learning, including policy planning for the economy's long-term competitiveness' *p*4. As Booyens [5] points out, this certainly fosters innovation. Similarly, *knowledge networks* amongst producers, creators and users provide for transfer of knowledge, which is an important determinant of innovation because it facilitates information exchange and collaboration.

Further, Booyens [5] asserts that to be meaningful, any innovation output should be economically viable, and this entails marketing and commercialisation of the innovation to attract *public support*. One also hopes that the financial gain is rechannelled into research and development. In sum, the output should be turned into an outcome. Oerlemans and Pretorius [68] have found no relationship between innovation outputs and innovation outcomes. Moving on from theory to practice, Cordeiro and Vieira [72] have discussed barriers to innovation in different European countries and one African country (Uganda). Generally, they point out internal (within the organisation) and external barriers (outside the organisation). More specifically, they point out the government regulatory environment, economic and financial factors, as well as human resources as constraints to innovation. **Table 2** shows a comparison of barriers to innovation across 14 selected countries including South Africa. Common barriers to innovation across countries include a limited or an absent regulatory environment and internal factors.

6.3 Established frameworks in innovation and entrepreneurship studies

Our discussion of established frameworks in innovation and entrepreneurship studies is incomplete if we do not include Schumpeter's 1940 theory of business cycles and development in which he points out innovation and entrepreneurship [70, 73] to

Country	Barriers to innovation
Brazil	Inadequate market access, risk in human resource allocation
Cyprus	Weak research and development activities, lack of funding, government bureaucracy
Czech Republic	Long payback periods, lack of legislation support, low consumer response, fear of risk
France	Lack of funding, resistance to innovation, low appetite for innovation from the consumer
Germany	Cost implications, bureaucracy within small and medium enterprises, lack of strategic co-operation between enterprises
Iran	Low funding on innovation also linked to high costs in innovation initiatives, poor response to innovation by the consumer and skill shortage
Italy	High financial risk, scarcity in information technology, regulatory requirements
Portugal	Organisational structures, absence of market leadership thinking, high risk associated with innovation, government regulation and lack of innovation skills
Spain	External environment, cost implications, knowledge deficiency on technology, lack of demand for innovative ideas
Switzerland	Limited skills, regulatory (legal) restrictions, lack of support in innovation education
Turkey	Inadequate policy support, lack of investment on innovation, skill shortages
United Kingdom	Risk aversion, poor market knowledge, difficulty in innovation timing
Uganda	Domestic market complications, non-supportive policies, bureaucratic regulatory requirements
South Africa	Lack of access to finance, rigid market structures, non-supportive regulatory environment, weak entrepreneurial culture, skill shortage (Wolf 2006, Herrington and others 2008)

Source: Cordeiro and Viera [72].

Table 2.
Barriers to innovation in different European countries [72].

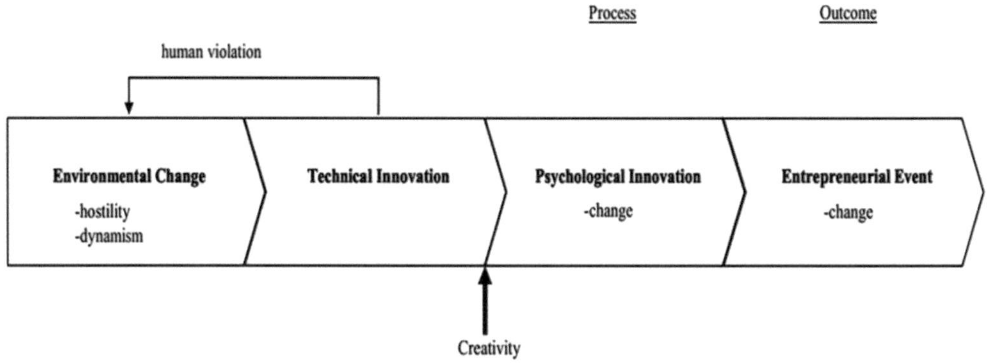

Figure 3.
Brazeal and Herbert's [75] model of the entrepreneurial process.

be the 'central feature of economic development' *p*96 and, as Sledzik [74] points out, the 'gales of creative destruction'. Further, an entrepreneur should reform and revolutionise production by exploiting inventions and untried technology. His framework is synonymous with the theories on disruptive innovation. **Figure 3** presents Brazeal and Herbert's [75] model of the entrepreneurial process, which links innovation and entrepreneurship. The emphasis is that innovation and entrepreneurship should complement each other because 'innovation is the source of entrepreneurship and entrepreneurship allows innovation to flourish' *p*13 [76].

There are also other established frameworks on innovation and entrepreneurship. For instance, Audretsch and Feldman [67] have argued that small and medium enterprises drive innovation in some industries. Further, Mahemba and De Bruijn [20] provide two useful frameworks—that is, *innovation and its adoption process* as well as *model of innovation activities of Small and Medium Entrepreneurs (SMEs)*. The former examines the key innovation process and activities, the summative products of innovation and the newness of innovation. Other important attributes of this framework include how the external environment influences generation and adoption of innovation. The latter – *model of innovation activities of SMEs* – examines how existing entrepreneurial characteristics and capabilities influence innovativeness. The other key attributes and variables include size of the market, knowledge and technological information.

Figure 4 is a model linking innovation to entrepreneurship. In this model, McFadzean and others [77] demonstrate how an organisation's performance is determined by its innovativeness and entrepreneurial capabilities via a combination of external and internal variables as well as the entrepreneur's attitudes and actions. The innovation process comprises idea generation, problem solving as well as implementation and diffusion. Whilst the entrepreneur component comprises strategic variables, external and internal variables, linking up innovation and entrepreneurship requires positive attitude, strategic vision and effective actions. Key to this framework is that innovation should be the output leading to entrepreneurship (the outcome), and yet in South Africa, there seems to be an emphasis on entrepreneurship.

Crossan and Apaydin's [1] determinants of innovation include four frameworks – that is, the upper echelon theory, resource-based view, dynamic capabilities and process theory – that one can use to interpret empirical results emanating from an innovation and entrepreneurial study. Hambrick and Mason [78] pioneered the upper echelon

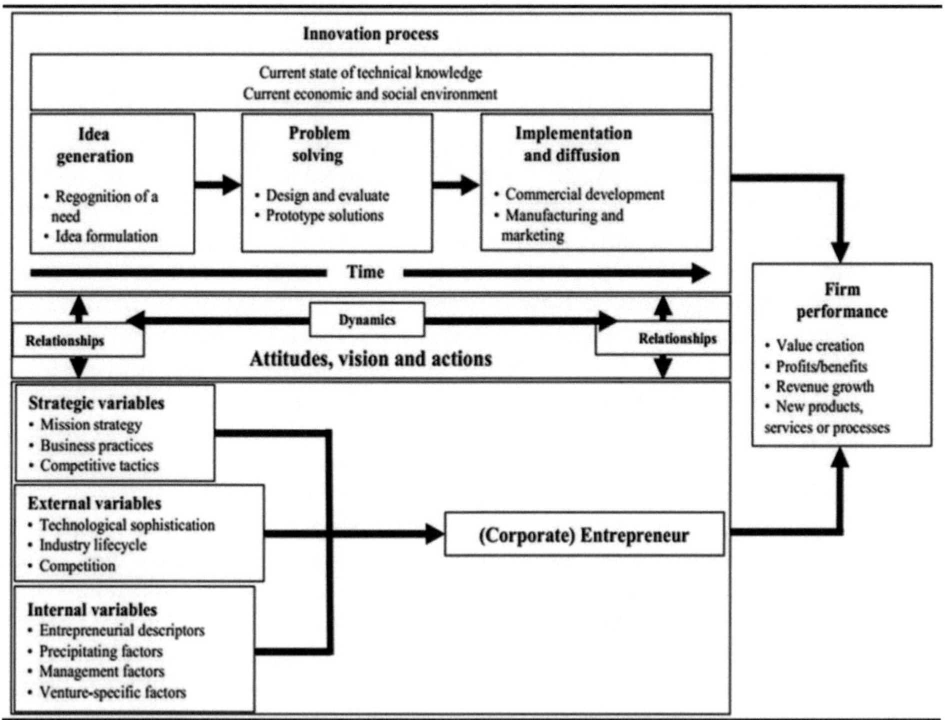

Source: McFadzean and others (2005)

Figure 4.
McFadzean and colleagues [77] depiction of the relationship between innovation and entrepreneurship.

theory, which postulates that one can use managerial characteristics, especially those of top management, to predict or estimate an organisation's performance. These characteristics, which include age, tenure and prior experience, influence how these individuals formulate and implement business strategies to influence the financial position of the organisation [79, 80]. However, Carpenter, Geletkanycz and Sanders [81] have argued that this framework is limited because it is centred on the demographic parameters of management. It inherently ignores other important aspects such as power, executive celebrity status and networks that also affect an organisation's financial performance. Further, some managers make decisions that reflect aspirations rather than past experience.

The resource-based view (RBV) probably dates back as far as 1930s. However, available documentation shows that it was originally coined by Edith Penrose in 1959 [82]. Later on, other scholars including Hamel and Prahalad [83] as well as Barney [84] strengthened its argument and incorporated it into strategic management. As the name suggests, the fundamental argument of this framework is that organisations use their internal strategic resources to improve their competitive advantage. These resources can be tangible or non-tangible and should be mobile and heterogeneous. Kraaijenbrink and colleagues [85] point out that the resources should be valuable, rare, costly to imitate and organised to capture value. The RBV provides for an immediate-face-validity, and it's simple to understand and implement. However, it does not emphasise the role of managers and focuses on internal resources and capabilities, therefore neglecting the contribution of the manager's ability to mobilise external resources [86]. Further, it is difficult to generalise this framework across different organisations, and it is mainly applicable to large organisations with a large market share and financial power [85].

The strategic management literature shows that Pisano, Teece and Shuen [87] coined the dynamic capabilities framework. It follows on the resource-based view to articulate that an organisation has the ability to integrate internal and external resources in response to changing business conditions. It provides for managers to'... extend, modify, and reconfigure existing operational capabilities into new ones that better match the environment' *p*239 [88]. When implemented in a stable conducive business environment, the framework enhances performance [89]. However, the framework provides for improving on competitiveness only, and even then, this is not guaranteed because there are other factors to consider, and results only show in the long run [90].

Harre and Madden [91] coined the process theory, which stipulates that (i.) similar inputs transformed by similar activities produce similar outputs and probably outcomes provided that (ii.) key, constant necessary conditions are present. Its use of probabilistic information on inputs and activities to predict certain outcomes under necessary supportive conditions [92] constitutes its strength. Therefore, as Van de Ven and Poole [93] have argued, a process identifies and describes generative mechanisms that lead to actual outputs and outcomes as well as anticipate diversions and accompanying contingencies. Unfortunately, the framework assumes unattainable perfect conditions and a conducive environment where inputs and activities are aligned. Another drawback is that the theory requires one to have an understanding of events and patterns in order to fully apply it.

7. Innovativeness in new business ventures: a conceptual framework

Eventually, the aim of this research is to detail innovativeness in new business ventures. To avoid being too ambitious, we narrow our target to Gauteng Province, being the economic hub of South Africa. Regardless, we can with caution apply the findings to other South African provinces and not only to the Southern African Development Community (SADC) but also to some parts of the African continent. This is more so with the content of this paper which articulates the theoretical fundamentals to conceptualise 'how' the empirical part of this research may be pursued. Obviously, unravelling that undertaking implies reviewing the literature to derive the conceptual framework that should guide the empirical part of this research. Effectively, a conceptual framework is a systematic summary of and decisions based on the literature reviewed in this paper. By default, this section also serves as the conclusion of the paper. **Figure 5** is a summarised visual representation of what we have discussed in this paper, and it also proposes how the empirical part of this research should proceed based on the literature reviewed.

Obviously, our pursuit is to decode determinants of low innovation in new business ventures in South Africa generally but more specifically Gauteng province. First of all, the physical research setting (Gauteng province) is the economic hub of not only South Africa but the African continent. As its name—place of gold—suggests, it is a mining region, and its economic base, which includes finance, manufacturing and technology sectors, was initially built around supporting its mining sector. There is no doubt that this province is a good candidate for such a research because it represents regions that have advanced in terms of innovation and entrepreneurship to provide us with data, information and knowledge on the status quo. Of course, we are mindful

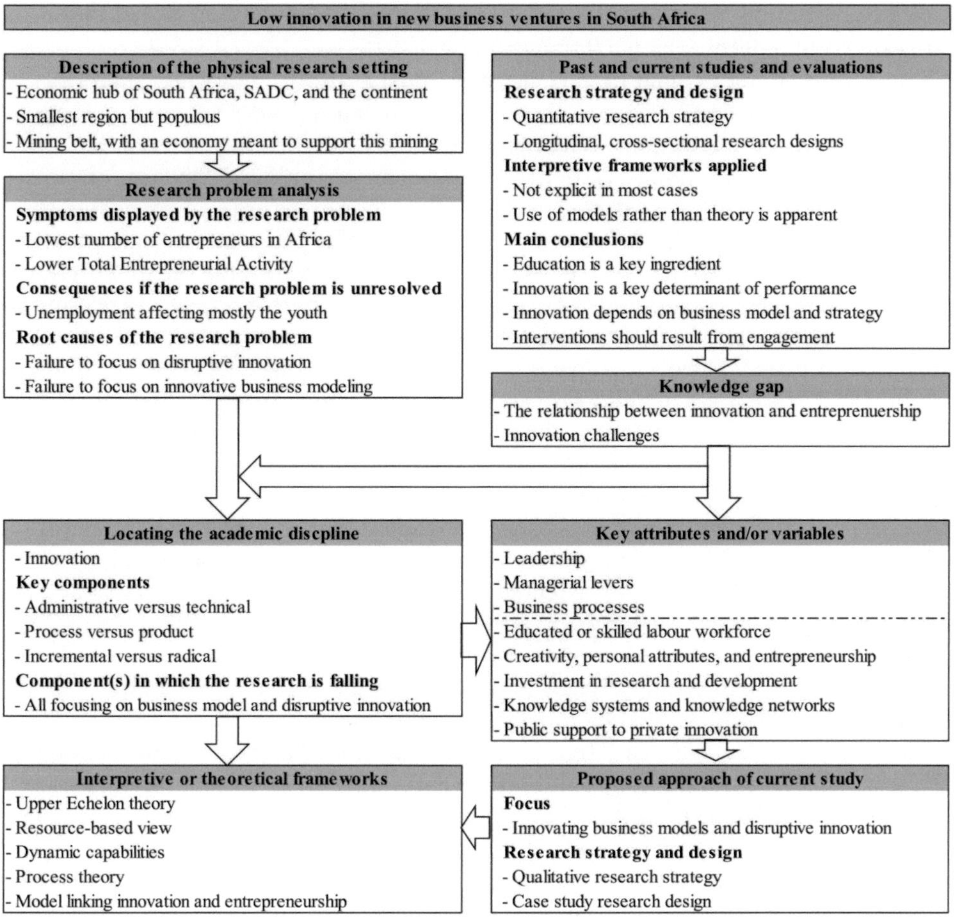

Figure 5.
A conceptual framework to guide empirical studies on disruptive innovation and innovative business models.

that focusing on a region that is less advanced would provide meaningful contribution on how we should advance. Regardless, the physical context or setting is important to detail because it affects development in general and specifically innovation as well as innovativeness in new business ventures. In our case, understanding the context helped with understanding the research problem as well as decide what would be the best research procedure and methods.

Second, despite being the fifth-most populous country in Africa and the third-largest in the Southern African Development Community (SADC) region as well as the economic hub of the continent, South Africa has the lowest number of entrepreneurs in Africa, and its Total Entrepreneurial Activity is low, such that status quo affects its economic growth and, therefore, employment especially amongst the youth. As a result, we cannot emphasise enough that innovation and entrepreneurship should be encouraged. The absence of entrepreneurial orientation – defined as an intervention that provides organisations to launch new ventures [94] – is not the problem. Rather it is the focus of these interventions. We propose that it is the failure to focus on disruptive innovation pitches ourselves against the leaders in innovation that makes us less competitive. Further, instead of focusing on innovative products and services, we should focus on innovative business models that seek to change the way we do business.

Third, though not explicit in most articles, most authors employed a quantitative research strategy and either a cross-sectional or a longitudinal research design. Similarly, the frameworks used to interpret their research findings are implicit, although it is clear that models rather than theories are employed. The two obvious points from the literature are that education is key to innovation and consequently entrepreneurship [26]. We, therefore, cannot divorce the poor state of mathematics and sciences in South Africa from innovation because they provide the much-required logic. Second, there is no doubt that innovation is key to performance and economic growth. However, and third, we should be mindful that this is not restricted to the innovation of products, services, technology, equipment, material and tools but more so to innovative business models, processes and portfolios – in short, how can we solve the problem of entrepreneurship failure as well as commercialise the products and services innovatively [1, 34, 35]. Lastly, the literature has focused on the person and not the context or the environment. Massa and Testa's [25] is a classic description of the African challenge. We have problems without solutions, on one hand, and, on the other, solutions without problems because there is little engagement, at least empirical and robust, with those affected. Interventions should be results-based. Key to this integration is that other than at a theoretical level, we are not sure about the relationship between innovation and entrepreneurship sufficiently enough to decode an effective, sustainable and efficient innovative business model. Further, what can we say are the challenges faced by those involved in innovation?

The literature—such as Christensen and Raynor [55], McFadzean and colleagues [77], Brem, [76], as well as Moses and others [31]—is quite clear that innovation is important for economic growth and employment creation for Gauteng Province if not the nation and the continent. Further, the literature has provided for understanding our research questions and exposing the knowledge gap and therefore, the two questions that empirical research should pursue. The first question – what factors can enhance disruptive innovation in Gauteng Province? – should be explicitly on disruptive innovation and not innovation in general or incremental. The second question – how can we innovate business models of small and medium entrepreneurs in Gauteng Province? – pursues ways of commercialising disruptive innovation products or services beyond the conventional ways of doing business.

Fourth, for purposes of proposing a framework for interpreting empirical results, we situate this study within innovation studies. Almost all the key processes – that is (i.) administrative versus technical, (ii.) process versus product and (iii.) incremental versus radical [1, 34] – are important. Much more specific, we should be looking at innovative business models as well as disruptive innovation.

Fifth, and merely a continuation of fourth, what attributes or variables should we focus on to interrogate innovative business models as well as disruptive innovation. Obviously, innovation has several attributes and variables, but we restrict ourselves to two sets. Crossan and Apaydin's [1] framework of organisational innovation provides useful attributes (leadership, managerial levels and business processes) that we can interrogate to study innovative business models especially managerial levels that provide for an explicit innovative strategy, mission, goals, and strategy of new business ventures aligned to their absorptive and desorptive capacities [52, 56]. The other set is Booyen's [5] factors to interrogate abilities to pursue disruptive innovation. These include educated or skilled labour workforce; creativity, personal attributes and entrepreneurship; investment in research and development; knowledge systems;

knowledge networks and public support to private innovation. With this in mind, we opt for a qualitative research strategy and a case study design to guide information collection, collation, processing and analysis. This is because our focus is not to extend but to detail the reasons underlying choice and processes of innovation ideals in business models as well as disruptive innovation.

Lastly, we propose employing the upper echelon theory, the resource-based view, dynamic capabilities and the process theory to interpret our research findings. To this list, we add the model linking innovation and entrepreneurship because it incorporates all the frameworks mentioned above on one platform. Ideally, we are looking to support disruptive innovation whose products and services can be commercialised using innovative business models.

8. Conclusion

Post-apartheid South Africa has probably put the wrong foot (entrepreneurship) in front of innovation, and yet the latter is fundamental. We argue that the emphasis should be innovation particularly disruptive and open innovation ahead of entrepreneurship. An emphasis on entrepreneurship is wrong because it implies defaulting to incremental innovation and hence competing with the pioneers of the product or service. It could be this lack of competitive edge that explains the high failure rate or discontinuance rate of South African new business ventures. The problem of innovation should be looked at in the light of the mathematics and science challenges the country is facing. Could it be that if we resolved this then innovation particularly disruptive innovation will also fall in place? Second, focusing on the product or service and neglecting innovation in the way we do business implies we can have an output but not the outcome. In this sense, the outcome should be commercialising the product or service arising out of innovation. In this case, then we need innovative business models that speak to the context. In this paper, we argue for disruptive innovation and innovative business models.

Acknowledgements

We are grateful to the WITS Business School (WBS) panel members of staff as well as the examiners of the research report where we have extracted this paper for their helpful comments. We would like to thank the editors and reviewers for helping us fine tune and reconcile our argument and perfect our write-up.

Conflict of interest

The authors declare that they have no financial or personal relationships which have inappropriately influenced them in this research or writing this article.

Author details

Clive Sithole[1] and Kambidima Wotela[2*]

1 WITS Business School, Johannesburg, South Africa

2 WITS School Governance, Johannesburg, South Africa

*Address all correspondence to: kambidima.wotela@wits.ac.za;
kambidima.wotela.wsg@gmail.com

References

[1] Crossan MM, Apaydin M. A multi-dimensional framework of organizational innovation: A systematic review of the literature. Journal of Management Studies. 2010;**47**(6):1154-1191

[2] Kruger ME, Millard SM, Pretorius M. Creativity, innovation and implementation: Management experience, venture size, life cycle stage, race and gender as moderators. South African Journal of Business Management. 2005;**36**(4):55-68

[3] Hasan M, Harris E. Entrepreneurship and innovation in e-commerce. Journal of Achievements in Materials and Manufacturing Engineering. 2009;**32**(1):92-97

[4] Drucker PF. The Essential Drucker. London: Routledge; 2020

[5] Booyens I. Are small, medium- and micro-sized enterprises engines of innovation? The reality in South Africa. Science and Public Policy. 2011;**38**(1):67-78

[6] Global Entrepreneur Monitor (GEM). Global Entrepreneurship Monitor 2021/2022 Global Report: Opportunity Amid Disruption. 2022. Available from: https://www.gemconsortium.org/reports/latest-global-report [Accessed: January 14, 2023]

[7] Levy Y, Ellis TJ. A systems approach to conduct an effective literature review in support of information systems research. Informing Science Journal. 2006;**9**:181-212

[8] Wotela K. Conceptualising conceptual frameworks in public and business management research. In: Proceedings of the 16th European Conference on Research Methodology for Business and Management Studies; 22-23 June 2017. Dublin: ACPI; 2017. pp. 370-380

[9] Kumar R. Research Methodology: A Step by Step Guide for Beginners. Los Angeles: Sage Publications; 2014

[10] Statistics South Africa. Mid-Year Population Estimates. Pretoria: Statistics South Africa; 2017

[11] Statistics South Africa. Four facts about our provincial economies. Pretoria: Statistics South Africa. 2018. Available from: https://www.statssa.gov.za/?p=12056 [Accessed: January 19, 2023

[12] Baumgardt J. Quality assurance challenges for private providers in post-school education and training in South Africa. University of South Africa, Unpublished doctoral thesis in Education Management, Pretoria; 2013

[13] Rogersons CM. Knowledge-based or smart regions in South Africa. South African Geographical Journal. 2001;**83**(1):34-47

[14] Lorentzen J. Provinces, City-Regions, and Innovation in South Africa. USA: Georgia Institute of Technology; 2008

[15] Pooe TK. South Africa's policy vision for black businesses–the role of entrepreneurship in development. In: Development in Modern Africa. London: Routledge; 2019. pp. 161-183

[16] Pangwa K, Wotela K. Towards a conceptual framework for the evaluability assessment of the Gauteng Science Park incubation Programme. In: Paper Presented at 5th Limpopo Chapter of the South African Association of

Public Administration and Management (SAAPAM) Annual Conference, 26-28 October 2016, Mokopane, South Africa. Limpopo: South African Association of Public Administration and Management; 2016

[17] Formica P. Stories of Innovation for the Millennial Generation: The Lynceus Long View. New York: Palgrave Macmillan; 2013

[18] Pérez-Luño A, Wiklund J, Cabrera RV. The dual nature of innovative activity: How entrepreneurial orientation influences innovation generation and adoption. Journal of Business Venturing. 2011;**26**(5):555-571

[19] Small and Medium Enterprises (SME) Growth Index. A country at the crossroads – toward better regulatory environment in South Africa. 2013. Available from: http://smegrowthindex.co.za/wp-content/uploads/2014/11/alert-digital.pdf [Accessed: June 26, 2019]

[20] Mahemba CM, Bruijn EJD. Innovation activities by small and medium-sized manufacturing enterprises in Tanzania. Creativity and Innovation Management. 2003;**12**(3):162-173

[21] Mone SD, Pop MD, Racolța-Paina ND. The "what" and "how" of marketing performance management. Management and Marketing. 2013;**8**(1):129-146

[22] Zott C, Amit R. Business model design and the performance of entrepreneurial firms. Organization Science. 2007;**18**(2):181-199

[23] Kropp F, Lindsay NJ, Shoham A. Entrepreneurial, market, and learning orientations and international entrepreneurial business venture performance in south African firms. International Marketing Review. 2006;**23**(5):504-523

[24] Purcarea I, Espinosa MMB, Apetrei A. Innovation and knowledge creation: Perspectives on the SMEs sector. Management Decision. 2013;**51**(5):1096-1107

[25] Massa S, Testa S. Innovation and SMEs: Misaligned perspectives and goals among entrepreneurs, academics, and policy makers. Technovation. 2008;**28**(7):393-407

[26] Robson P, Obeng B, Haugh H. Entrepreneurship and innovation in Ghana: Enterprising Africa. Small Business Economics. 2009;**32**:331-350

[27] Anokhin S, Wincent J. Start-up rates and innovation: A cross-country examination. Journal of International Business Studies. 2012;**43**(1):41-60

[28] Wong PK, Ho YP, Autio E. Entrepreneurship, innovation and economic growth: Evidence from GEM data. Small business Economics. 2005;**24**(3):335-350

[29] Shane S. Why encouraging more people to become entrepreneurs is bad public policy. Small business Economics. 2009;**33**(2):141-149

[30] Radas S, Božić L. The antecedents of SME innovativeness in an emerging transition economy. Technovation. 2009;**29**(6-7):438-450

[31] Moses C, Sithole MM, Blankley W, Labadarios D, Makelane H, Nkobole N. The state of innovation in South Africa: Findings from the south African National Innovation Survey. South African Journal of Science. 2012;**108**(7-8):15-20

[32] Autio E, Kenney M, Mustar P, Siegel D, Wright M. Entrepreneurial

innovation: The importance of context. Research Policy. 2014;**43**(7):1097-1108

[33] Ndabeni LL. Small medium and micro Enterprises in South Africa's National System of innovation. In: Preliminary Report Prepared for the Global Research Network for Learning, Innovation and Competence Building Systems. Brazil: Economics Institute of the Federal University of Rio de Janeiro; 2012

[34] Gopalakrishnan S, Damanpour F. A review of innovation research in economics, sociology and technology management. Omega. 1997;**25**(1):15-28

[35] Wang CL, Ahmed PK. The development and validation of the organisational innovativeness construct using confirmatory factor analysis. European Journal of Innovation Management. 2004;**7**(4):303-313

[36] Bogers M. The sources of process innovation in user firms: An exploration of the antecedents and impact of non-R&D innovation and learning-by-doing. Ecole Polytechnique Fédérale de Lausanne, Unpublished doctoral thesis, Lausanne; 2009

[37] Hadjimanolis A, Dickson K. Innovation strategies of SMEs in Cyprus, a small developing country. International Small Business Journal. 2000;**18**(4):62-79

[38] Freeman C. Economics of Industrial Innovation. Routledge; 2013

[39] Miles RE, Snow CC, Meyer AD, Coleman Jr HJ. Organizational strategy, structure, and process. Academy of Management Review. 1978;**3**(3):546-562

[40] Miller D, Friesen PH. A longitudinal study of the corporate life cycle. Management Science. 1984;**30**(10):1161-1183

[41] Urban GL, Hauser JR. Design and Marketing of New Products. Englewood Cliffs: Prentice Hall; 1980

[42] Chesbrough H. Business model innovation: Opportunities and barriers. Long range Planning. 2010;**43**(2-3):354-363

[43] Markides C. Disruptive innovation: In need of better theory. Journal of Product Innovation Management. 2006;**23**(1):19-25

[44] Shirky C. Here Comes Everybody: The Power of Organizing without Organizations. New York: Penguin; 2008

[45] Andries P, Debackere K. Adaptation and performance in new businesses: Understanding the moderating effects of independence and industry. Small Business Economics. 2007;**29**(1-2):81-99

[46] Teece DJ. Business models, business strategy and innovation. Long Range Planning. 2010;**43**(2-3):172-194

[47] Delmar F, Shane S. Does business planning facilitate the development of new ventures? Strategic Management Journal. 2003;**24**(12):1165-1185

[48] George G, Bock AJ. The business model in practice and its implications for entrepreneurship research. Entrepreneurship Theory and Practice. 2011;**35**(1):83-111

[49] Chesbrough H. Open innovation: A new paradigm for understanding industrial innovation. Open Innovation: Researching a New Paradigm. 2006;**400**:0-19

[50] Gassman O, Enkel E, Chesbrough H. The future of open innovation. R&D Management. 2010;**40**:3

[51] Bianchi M, Campodall'Orto S, Frattini F, Vercesi P. Enabling open

innovation in small-and medium-sized enterprises: How to find alternative applications for your technologies. R&D Management. 2010;**40**(4):414-431

[52] Hossain M. A review of literature on open innovation in small and medium-sized enterprises. Journal of Global Entrepreneurship Research. 2015;**5**(1):6

[53] Thomond P, Herzberg T, Lettice F. Disruptive innovation: Removing the innovators dilemma. In: British Academy of Management Annual Conference: Knowledge into Practice. 2003

[54] Hamel G. Leading the Revolution. Boston: Harvard Business School Press; 2000

[55] Christensen CM, Raynor ME, Anthony SD. Six Keys to Building New Markets by Unleashing Disruptive Innovation. EEUU: Harvard Management; 2003

[56] Tipping P, Zefran E. Open innovation: The absorptive and desorptive capacities. Journal of Management Studies. 1995;**23**(6):66-88

[57] Lichtenthaler U, Lichtenthaler E. A capability-based framework for open innovation: Complementing absorptive capacity. Journal of Management Studies. 2009;**46**(8):1315-1338

[58] Hausman A. Innovativeness among small businesses: Theory and propositions for future research. Industrial Marketing Management. 2005;**34**(8):773-782

[59] Carayannis EG, Campbell DF, editors. Knowledge Creation, Diffusion, and Use in Innovation Networks and Knowledge Clusters: A Comparative Systems Approach across the United States, Europe, and Asia. Westport: Greenwood Publishing Group; 2006

[60] Rosenbusch N, Brinckmann J, Bausch A. Is innovation always beneficial? A meta-analysis of the relationship between innovation and performance in SMEs. Journal of Business Venturing. 2011;**26**(4):441-457

[61] Geissdoerfer M, Vladimirova D, Van Fossen K, Evans S. Product, service, and business model innovation: A discussion. Procedia Manufacturing. 2018;**21**:165-172

[62] Cooper RG, Edgett SJ, Kleinschmidt EJ. New product portfolio management: Practices and performance. Journal of Product Innovation Management. 1999;**16**(4):333-351

[63] Bessant JR. High-Involvement Innovation: Building and Sustaining Competitive Advantage through Continuous Change. Chichester: Wiley; 2003

[64] Adams R, Bessant J, Phelps R. Innovation management measurement: A review. International Journal of Management Reviews. 2006;**8**(1):21-47

[65] Madrid-Guijarro A, Garcia D, Van Auken H. Barriers to innovation among Spanish manufacturing SMEs. Journal of Small Business Management. 2009;**47**(4):465-488

[66] Maré DC. What do endogenous growth models contribute?. Wellington: Motu Economic and Public Policy Research Working Paper 04-04; 2004

[67] Audretsch DB, Feldman MP. Knowledge Spillovers and the Geography of Innovation. In Handbook of Regional and Urban Economics. Vol. 4. Elsevier; 2004. pp. 2713-2739

[68] Oerlemans LA, Pretorius MW. Some views on determinants of innovative outcomes of south African firms: An exploratory analysis using firm-level

data. South African Journal of Science. 2006;**102**(11):589-593

[69] Marcati A, Guido G, Peluso AM. The role of SME entrepreneurs' innovativeness and personality in the adoption of innovations. Research Policy. 2008;**37**(9):1579-1590

[70] Schumpeter JA. Essays: On entrepreneurs, innovations, business cycles and the evolution of capitalism. In: Clemence RV, editor. Reading. Addison-Wesley; 1951

[71] Wolf S. Encouraging innovation and productivity growth in Africa to create decent jobs. In: Paper Presented at DPRU/TIPS Conference on Accelerated and Shared Growth in South Africa: Determinants, Constraints, and Opportunities; 18-20 October 2006. Johannesburg: DPRU/TIPS; 2006. pp. 1-20

[72] Cordeiro A, Vieira FD. Barriers to Innovation in SMEs: An International Comparison. In: II Conferencia Internacional de Integração do Design, Engenharia e Gestão para a inovação Florianópolis; 21-23 October 2012. Brasil; 2012

[73] Sweezy PM. Professor Schumpeter's theory of innovation. The Review of Economic Statistics. 1943:93-96

[74] Śledzik K. Schumpeter's view on innovation and entrepreneurship. In: Hittmar S, editor. Management Trends in Theory and Practice. Slovakia: Faculty of Management Science and Informatics, University of Zilina & Institute of Management by University of Zilina; 2013

[75] Brazeal DV, Herbert TT. The genesis of entrepreneurship. Entrepreneurship Theory and Practice. 1999;**23**(3):29-46

[76] Brem A. Linking innovation and entrepreneurship–literature overview and introduction of a process-oriented framework. International Journal of Entrepreneurship and Innovation Management. 2011;**14**(1):6-35

[77] McFadzean E, O'Loughlin A, Shaw E. Corporate entrepreneurship and innovation part 1: The missing link. European Journal of Innovation Management. 2005;**8**(3):350-372

[78] Hambrick DC, Mason PA. Upper echelons: The organization as a reflection of its top managers. Academy of Management Review. 1984;**9**(2):193-206

[79] Nielsen S. Top management team diversity: A review of theories and methodologies. International Journal of Management Reviews. 2010;**12**(3):301-316

[80] Ting IWK, Azizan NAB, Kweh QL. Upper echelon theory revisited: The relationship between CEO personal characteristics and financial leverage decision. Procedia-Social and Behavioral Sciences. 2015;**195**:686-694

[81] Carpenter MA, Geletkanycz MA, Sanders WG. Upper echelons research revisited: Antecedents, elements, and consequences of top management team composition. Journal of Management. 2004;**30**(6):749-778

[82] Penrose E, Penrose ET. The Theory of the Growth of the Firm. Oxford: Oxford University Press; 2009

[83] Hamel G, Prahalad CK. Strategic intent. Mckinsey Quarterly. 1990;**1**:36-61

[84] Barney J. Firm resources and sustained competitive advantage. Journal of Management. 1991;**17**(1):99-120

[85] Kraaijenbrink J, Spender JC, Groen AJ. The resource-based view: A review and

assessment of its critiques. Journal of Management. 2010;**36**(1):349-372

[86] Warnier V, Weppe X, Lecocq X. Extending resource-based theory: Considering strategic, ordinary and junk resources. Management Decision. 2013;**51**(7):1359-1379

[87] Teece DJ, Pisano G, Shuen A. Dynamic capabilities and strategic management. Strategic Management Journal. 1997;**18**(7):509-533

[88] Pavlou PA, El Sawy OA. Understanding the elusive black box of dynamic capabilities. Decision Sciences. 2011;**42**(1):239-273

[89] Drnevich PL, Kriauciunas AP. Clarifying the conditions and limits of the contributions of ordinary and dynamic capabilities to relative firm performance. Strategic Management Journal. 2011;**32**(3):254-279

[90] Barreto I. Dynamic capabilities: A review of past research and an agenda for the future. Journal of Management. 2010;**36**(1):256-280

[91] Harré R, Madden EH. Causal Powers: A Theory of Natural Necessity. Oxford: Basil Blackwell; 1975

[92] Langley A. Strategies for theorizing from process data. Academy of Management Review. 1999;**24**(4):691-710

[93] Van de Ven AH, Poole MS. Explaining development and change in organizations. Academy of Management Review. 1995;**20**(3):510-540

[94] Dess GG, Lumpkin GT. The role of entrepreneurial orientation in stimulating effective corporate entrepreneurship. Academy of Management Perspectives. 2005;**19**(1):147-156

Chapter 2

Business Intelligence: An Important Tool to Develop Dynamic Capabilities and Sustainable Innovation in the Digital Age

Abdeslam Hassani and Hussam Al Halbusi

Abstract

While the issue of business intelligence is rapidly gaining popularity across a wide range of domains, the majority of research treats it as a single capability or technique, such as big data analytics capability. However, as a tool for Big Data Decision-making or technique for enhancing operational research technique, there is still a low amount of work that examines business intelligence as a tool to develop dynamic capabilities of the organization and to contribute to sustainable innovation, in particular in the digital age. Therefore, to address this gap, this chapter aims to discuss how organizations can use technologies, including business intelligence as a tool for creating new knowledge, which in turn helps organizations to improve their dynamic capabilities and achieve sustainable innovation. Recognizing how these firms' dynamic capabilities are started building, achieved sustained, enlarged, utilized, evolved, and phased out in phrases of their constituent micro-foundations. So, this study suggests business intelligence as a process that helps organizations collect and transform data into information and knowledge, which contributes to building dynamic capabilities. It is important for managers to understand how these firms' dynamic capabilities are started building, achieved sustained, enlarged, utilized, evolved, and phased out in phrases of their constituent micro-foundations.

Keywords: business intelligence, dynamic capabilities, innovation, digitalization, sustainability

1. Introduction

Over the last several years, scholars and practitioners have recognized, considered, and identified how increased digitalization and datafication of social action facilitates new opportunities for arranging and changing patterns of organizations [1–3]. Among all businesses have an ongoing shift towards further digital forms of work in recent times. Digitalization can indeed be seen as the renovation of controller inputs into digital forms [4, 5]. Nonetheless, the digital revolution changes organizational capabilities by removing or reducing material constrictions related to work, such as time, space, location, or capital requirements. Whilst the work and information exchange could be digitized, it is further appropriate to consider trying to organize as an implementation of change [5, 6]. Once organizations use the digital format nature of work to produce unique forms, they are digitalizing the organization which include increasingly distributed and flexible work arrangements [7]. The automation of administrative task system applications, the adaptation of knowledge management systems [8], and the use of businesses as networking sites [9]. Enterprises can significantly enhance the amount of data that is transparent and inclusive because digitization drives the marginal cost of producing information goods to near zero and digital storage costs continue falling. Digital technology for contemporary businesses is a procedure of digitalization that many see as required to pursue innovation and remain competitive [10, 11].

The advancing technological accessibility enabled by a variety of networks and electronic tools delivers the facilities for digital data to be transmitted comfortably. As the fundamental network process that links individuals are becoming more rigorous, so will expectations for social and organizational internet access [12]. Furthermore, as demonstrated in prior research, the vastly increased accessibility of digital data allows individuals within companies to anticipate ever more social, and business interconnection since work activities are regarded as easily transportable [13, 14], compelling companies to expand the economy in their techniques to overcome to require to ensure levels of information technology connectivity. In simple, digital data contributes to increased requirements for technological and human integration, in which the compound process is repeated to the place where things in companies expect to be continuously connected to each other at all points of time [15].

Digital technologies can provide organizations with rapid access, enormous opportunities, and challenges [16]. Given the growing influences and reliance on digital technologies and applications in various market segments, the relevance and significance of implementing strategic understanding in organizations have a larger effect than ever on the development and sustainability of achieving competitive advantage and value [17, 18]. However, apart from the application of strategic understanding, the previous research on digitally enabled conceptualizations, for example, cloud computing, Internet of things (IoT), big data, and business intelligence sees them as valuable processes for solving challenges, which are frequently linked to attaining and sustaining value for stakeholders [19, 20]. Otherwise, technological innovations and human movement have consistently aided in the management of strategic knowledge and capabilities in businesses. Indeed, some intelligence tools and practices such as business and competitive intelligence can help firms create new knowledge, which contributes to developing dynamic capabilities within firms [21, 22].

Some previous research (e.g., [23–25] investigated the relationships between certain components related to business intelligence such as the analytical capacity on one side, and the dynamic capabilities, and performance of the organization on the other side. However, there is still a lack of research that examines the impact of business intelligence on certain internal mechanisms of company performance [26], in particular on sustainable innovation. This paper attempts to fill this research gap by examining how business intelligence can contribute to sustainable innovation through dynamic capabilities. This study aims to explore the role of business intelligence in developing dynamic capabilities and its direct and/or indirect contribution to innovation activities and the sustainable organizational performance of companies. More specifically, this study aims to answer the following research question:

Q1—How does business intelligence contributes to the development of dynamic capabilities and, therefore, to the sustainable innovation of organizations?

This paper attempt to explain how business intelligence can help to develop technological dynamic capabilities, which in turn contribute to sustainable innovation. Although this paper presents only a theoretical study, it proposes a research model which can guide managers to make the best choices regarding investment in technological resources such as business intelligence.

The remainder of this chapter is structured as follows: (1) this introduction, describing the relevance of the research topic and its context; (2) the definition of business intelligence; (3) the relationship between business intelligence, dynamic capabilities, and sustainable innovation; (4) the implications; (5) the limitations and future research, and; (6) the conclusion.

2. Business intelligence

In recent years, there has been an increasing interest in intelligence activities such as business intelligence, competitive intelligence, and artificial intelligence. In this section, we choose to highlight the need for organizations to build dynamic capabilities by using technologies especially, business intelligence, which helps them to be more competitive and innovative [27].

Business intelligence is a concept that emerged in the early 1970s when transactional information systems could not help managers make decisions. This weakness spurred the development of a set of tools and techniques based on advanced algorithms to process data faster to achieve organizational goals [28]. New decision-support information systems have enabled companies to process large volumes of data requiring rapid storage and access [29]. In their comprehensive literature review, [30] view business intelligence as a combination of policies, processes, cultures, and technologies used to store, manipulate, and analyze data. In addition, four main steps characterize business intelligence: system sources, data acquisition, data warehouse, and reporting and analysis [31, 32].

From another perspective, business intelligence is an umbrella term that can also be defined as a set of data aggregation processing methods from different departments such as marketing, sales, human resources, and finance that assists executives in decision-making [33]. For a long time, data related to different disciplines existed within organizations without being well leveraged. In addition, the emergence of new technologies has greatly contributed to flooding businesses with massive and varied data, which required a tool to help integrate, store, and analyze data in order to create information and knowledge for decision-making. Business intelligence's main role is to transform data into information, then into knowledge and action [34]. To this end, it is relevant to distinguish between information and knowledge. According to [35], information is factual; it refers to a set of numbers, statistics, and scattered data, among others, on people, and companies, while knowledge is a set of information that has been filtered, analyzed, and then implemented. In the same vein, [36, 37] report that knowledge is the richest form of information. For these authors, knowledge is a set of information on a given subject, which has been interpreted, reformulated, and put into action by an individual based on his expertise and prior knowledge.

3. Business intelligence, dynamic capabilities, and sustainable innovation

Previous studies have reported that knowledge is a key lever for organizational learning, innovation, and developing a set of organizational capabilities, such as dynamic capabilities [38]. For this reason, [39, 40] suggest integrating knowledge flows and organizational learning as a dimension of dynamic capabilities. According to this perspective, intelligence tools and techniques based on information collection, analysis, and dissemination contribute to knowledge generation [41] and the development of dynamic capabilities [42, 43].

The dynamic capabilities approach is now the dominant framework in strategic management for explaining the reconfiguration of resources and competencies through which organizations can respond to changes in their environment and innovate [44]. The dynamic capabilities consist of three categories, identifying and assessing opportunities (sensing), mobilizing resources to take advantage of the identified opportunity (seizing), and continuously reconfiguring resources (transforming) [45]. Dynamic capabilities can be defined as "the firm's ability to integrate, build, and reconfigure internal and external resources or competencies to address, and possibly shape, rapidly changing business environments" [46, 47]. This definition highlights the importance of reconfiguration of organizational resources that help managers to identify opportunities and threats then act quickly to adjust to frequent changes in the external environment.

A number of researchers consider the relationship between dynamic capabilities and technologies as a bidirectional relation. Indeed, on the one hand, and on the other hand, technologies including analytic tools contribute to developing dynamic capabilities, and the relevance of sensing and learning capabilities can be seen as a trigger of technologies capabilities [47]. In the era of advanced technologies that have invaded all organizations, many researchers consider information technologies capabilities, such as the expertise of staff in technical knowledge, the flexibility of the information technologies infrastructure, and the ability to manage information technologies one among dynamic capabilities dimensions [48]. In the same sense, [49] point out that the development of new technological capabilities helps managers to adapt quickly to the turbulence of the environment [50] suggests that information technologies grant organizations the capacity to transform and bring out new knowledge, which promotes the improvement of their dynamic capabilities. Indeed, to manage dynamic data and information, organizations necessitate having analytic capabilities and a governance plan to maximize value [51].

There have been several types of research reports that business intelligence and dynamic capabilities are significantly correlated in the area of business and management studies. Although most researchers in the field consider business intelligence a single capability, such as Big Data Analytics Capability [52], a tool of Big Data Decision-making [53], or a technique for enhancing Operational Research [37], it can be considered a trigger of dynamic capabilities [19]. Business intelligence plays an important role in creating knowledge and developing dynamics capabilities within firms. It improves the collection of relevant information on the needs of customers and external partners, which helps develop organizations' sensing capacity [40].

Previous studies highlight several advantages of dynamic capabilities within organizations [53] reports that the dynamic capabilities approach helps managers to create a competitive advantage. In the same vein, the dynamic capabilities strategy is asserted to be an encouraging approach to improving the understanding of critical innovation management for environmental sustainability [54]. Businesses should start to consider their fundamental actions in order to integrate, coordinate, build, and reconfigure their resources and competencies in the context of external sustainable development innovations [11]. Dynamic capabilities enable a company to align its resources and competencies with strategic environmental policies and the general business environment. To look at it another way, a company's dynamic capabilities evaluate its capacity and willingness to implement these changes in its competencies and resources in order to participate in the transformation to a more sustainable industry [44, 55]. Thus, it highly suggests that dynamic capabilities be evaluated particularly for various tasks because there are numerous multiple kinds of dynamic capabilities for carrying out various tasks, ranging from new product development to post-acquisition incorporation (e.g., see [46]).

Giving to past studies, businesses are indeed successful in bringing new technologies and products for environmental protection to the industry when they establish and organize their innovation capability around sustainable solutions [56, 57]. The implementation of clean and energy-efficient technologies is dependent on businesses' opportunity to develop dynamic capabilities for this function. As a result, more studies on businesses' dynamic capabilities for environmentally responsible advancements have indeed required the kind of dynamic capabilities that should be developed to successfully overcome starting to emerge emerging issues [58]. Therefore, continued studies make the argument that, while much progress was made in understanding organizational capabilities, the reasoning behind these shared occurrences takes account of these constructs' micro-level, or "micro-foundations." A micro foundations method is concerned with unpacking dynamic capabilities in terms of fundamental different elements [50, 59]. Dynamic capabilities should always be described in terms of organizational structures and managerial ways of implementing business models. The managerial and organizational practices related to how things are done in businesses are also known as procedures or patterns of current practice and learning, [6, 60] characterizes micro foundations as "distinct skills, processes, procedures, organizational structures, decision rules, and disciplines" that serve as the overall organizational underpinning for resources and capabilities.

To attain sustainable growth, businesses are progressively considering the importance of the building and advancement of environmentally sustainable innovations [4, 61]. Sustainable innovation is considered an innovative and principal characteristic of business operations that confront the existing system in order to develop innovative products and processes that not only produce value-added economic performance but also advantage the environmental ecosystems [62]. For instance, immaculate technology solutions are indeed a type of environmentally sustainable innovation that aims to minimize dependence on renewable sources while also promoting environmental sustainability through the development of many more produces more power advanced technology [63]. Sustainable innovation as a business enabler allows businesses to implement sustainable development concerns regarding their techniques whereas strengthening their competitiveness [64]. Since a wide range of stakeholders is involved in the design process, incorporating environmental policies complicates businesses' innovation strategies. The sophistication of the innovation process influences everything from concept development to marketing practices [65]. According to [66, 67], this complexity is triggered by the robust and sophisticated innovation of operations and product higher-level technology and the ambiguity and variety of the technological and business domains in which businesses usually start competing.

This unpredictability complicates strategic directions, particularly one's innovation schemes and performance because this requires to face changes and be able to adapt the business's capabilities to its environment [15, 68]. Given to [69], environmental sustainability innovation regularly encompasses a departure from the existing body of knowledge and is therefore competence-destroying. Sustainable innovation frequently necessitates a disruptive technological transformation or a complete solution overhaul

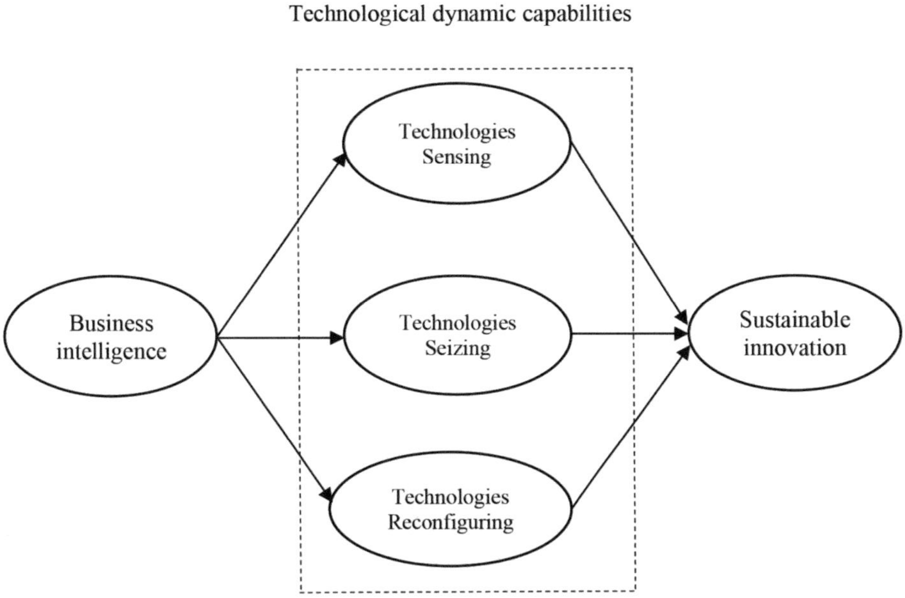

Figure 1.
Research model.

[70]. Also, [71] contends that environmentally sustainable innovation varieties from responsibility affect so otherwise to doing completely diverse things. As a result, mainstream, market-driven perspectives to advancement are insufficient for smartly improving and maintaining innovation for environmental sustainability [72, 73].

As we mentioned above, the digital transformation age represents a set of opportunities that should be sensed and seized. To do so, firms must reconfigure their technological resources and mobilize their organizational capabilities, including business intelligence [74, 75]. Indeed, business intelligence as a tool for collecting and analyzing information helps to identify opportunities, predict market trends, and helps to anticipate external changes by reconfiguring internal resources, particularly technological resources. In the same manner, [76] reports that to take advantage of emerging big data opportunities, firms must continually renew and reconfigure their technological resources. Based on the discussion above, we propose the research model below (**Figure 1**).

4. Implications

Some previous research investigated the relationships between certain components related to business intelligence such as the analytical capacity on one side, the dynamic capabilities, and the performance of the organization on the other side. However, there is still a lack of research that examines the impact of business intelligence on certain internal mechanisms of company performance [26, 77], in particular on sustainable innovation. This paper contributes to fill this research gap by examining how business intelligence can contribute to sustainable innovation through dynamic capabilities. It aims to explore the role of business intelligence in the development of dynamic capabilities and its direct and/or indirect contribution to innovation activities and the sustainable organizational performance of companies. Precisely, this study proposes a research model which shows the importance of business intelligence to build the technological dynamic capabilities that led to sustainable innovation. Although this paper presents only a theoretical study, it proposes a research model which can guide managers to make the best choices regarding investment in technological resources such as business intelligence [78].

Practically, to achieve global performance and be more competitive, firms' managers need to question the ability of their organizations to innovate, which leads them to mobilize the dynamic capabilities for developing innovative products and services that lead to disrupting and energizing the market [79]. The research of [68, 80] using a survey of 175 Greek companies highlights that dynamic capabilities play a mediator role in the relationships between business intelligence and innovation (incremental and radical innovation). Given the importance of business intelligence in creating new knowledge [81, 82] and its contribution to developing dynamic capabilities [71], which lead to sustainable innovation, firms need to consider and give more attention to investing in digitalization and analytical technologies. Dynamic capabilities help firms to reconfigure resources continuously and achieve sustainable growth [6, 9, 83].

5. Limitations and future research

This study presents some limitations that can be seen as an opportunity for further research. First, the proposed research model in this paper may be considered in the future more qualitative and quantitative empirical investigations can be developed in the future to expand and validate our recommendations. As this will help to improve the understanding related to sustainable innovation, as it's an important component of the economy of all countries. Second, our paper does not specify the context if it is in large companies or SMEs because business intelligence and the technological reconfiguration of resources require a large investment, which it's limited in the SMEs context. Therefore, future research could examine and compare the research model by considering the firm as a control variable. Finally, researchers can also widen and strengthen this research area by recognizing businesses' strategy catalysts, assessing their platform-based innovation management levels, and analyzing the influence on their performance, such as revenues development and customer attrition. Second, Future research may list the appropriate capabilities (e.g., digital analysis, network orchestrating, value co-creation skills) required for businesses to operate platform-based PSI systems, improving our knowledge of platform-based servitization's operational characteristics.

6. Conclusion

In the age of digitalization, new technologies influence organizational capabilities, which allow the firm's managers to develop prospecting and foresight techniques and practices to face environmental changing. Among these practices, many studies suggest business intelligence as a process that helps organizations collect and transform data into information and knowledge, which contributes to building dynamic capabilities. As mentioned above, dynamic capabilities refer to an organization's ability to voluntarily create, expand, or change its resource base to address threats associated with the volatility of the business environment. Therefore, it is important for managers to understand how these firms' dynamic capabilities are started building, achieved sustained, enlarged, utilized, evolved, and phased out in phrases of their constituent micro-foundations [84, 85].

Acknowledgements

The authors thank Université de Québec à Trois-Rivières for supporting this research.

Conflict of interest

No potential conflict of interest was reported by the author.

Author details

Abdeslam Hassani[1*] and Hussam Al Halbusi[2]

1 École de gestion, Université de Québec à Trois-Rivières, Trois-Rivières, Canada

2 Management Department, Ahmed Bin Mohammed Military College, Doha, Qatar

*Address all correspondence to: abdeslam.hassani@uqtr.ca

References

[1] Kim S, Choi B, Lew Y. Where is the age of digitalization heading? The meaning, characteristics, and implications of contemporary digital transformation. Sustainability. 2021;**13**(16):8909

[2] Trischler J, Westman Trischler J. Design for experience—A public service design approach in the age of digitalization. Public Management Review. 2022;**24**(8):1251-1270

[3] Al Halbusi H et al. Exploring social media adoption in small and medium enterprises in Iraq: Pivotal role of social media network capability and customer involvement. Technology Analysis & Strategic Management. 2022;**2022**:1-18

[4] Grybauskas A, Stefanini A, Ghobakhloo M. Social sustainability in the age of digitalization: A systematic literature review on the social implications of industry 4.0. Technology in Society. 2022;**2022**:101997

[5] Ghosh S, Hughes M, Hodgkinson I, Hughes P. Digital transformation of industrial businesses: A dynamic capability approach. Technovation. 2022;**113**:102414

[6] Chen Y et al. Building data-driven dynamic capabilities to arrest knowledge hiding: A knowledge management perspective. Journal of Business Research. 2022;**139**:1138-1154

[7] van Kersbergen K, Vis B. Digitalization as a policy response to social acceleration: Comparing democratic problem solving in Denmark and the Netherlands. Government Information Quarterly. 2022;**2022**:101707

[8] Bamel U, Kumar S, Lim W, Bamel N, Meyer N. Managing the dark side of digitalization in the future of work: A fuzzy TISM approach. Journal of Innovation and Knowledge. 2022;**7**(4):100275

[9] Fuegener A, Grahl J, Gupta A, Ketter W. Cognitive challenges in human–artificial intelligence collaboration: Investigating the path toward productive delegation. Information Systems Research. 2022;**33**(2):678-696

[10] Bartschat M, Cziehso G, Hennig-Thurau T. Searching for word of mouth in the digital age: Determinants of consumers' uses of face-to-face information, internet opinion sites, and social media. Journal of Business Research. 2022;**141**:393-409

[11] Al Halbusi H. Digital entrepreneurship and personal resilience on new business models in the 21st century. In: Handbook of Research on Entrepreneurship and Organizational Resilience During Unprecedented Times. IGI Global; 2023. pp. 331-351

[12] Lee SM, Trimi S. Convergence innovation in the digital age and in the COVID-19 pandemic crisis. Journal of Business Research. 2021;**123**:14-22

[13] Tsou HT, Chen JS. How does digital technology usage benefit firm performance? Digital transformation strategy and organisational innovation as mediators. Technology Analysis & Strategic Management. 2021;**2021**:1-2

[14] Blanka C, Krumay B, Rueckel D. The interplay of digital transformation and employee competency: A design science approach. Technological Forecasting and Social Change. 2022;**178**:121575

[15] Spieth P, Röth T, Clauss T, Klos C. Technological frames in the digital age: Theory, measurement instrument, and future research areas. Journal of Management Studies. 2021;**58**(7):1962-1993

[16] Zallio M, Clarkson P. Designing the Metaverse: A study on inclusion, diversity, equity, accessibility and safety for digital immersive environments. Telematics and Informatics. 2022;**2022**:101909

[17] Venkitachalam K, Schiuma G. Strategic knowledge management (SKM) in the digital age–insights and possible research directions. Journal of Strategy and Management. 2022;**15**(2):169-174

[18] Alshallaqi M et al. Resistance to digital innovation in low-income populations: The case of university Student's resistance to using digital productivity applications. Frontiers in Psychology. 2022;**2022**:5547

[19] Weaven S, Quach S, Thaichon P, Frazer L, Billot K, Grace D. Surviving an economic downturn: Dynamic capabilities of SMEs. Journal of Business Research. 2021;**128**:109-123

[20] Banmairuroy W, Kritjaroen T, Homsombat W. The effect of knowledge-oriented leadership and human resource development on sustainable competitive advantage through organizational innovation's component factors: Evidence from Thailand's new S-curve industries. Asia Pacific Management Review. 2022;**27**(3):200-209

[21] Côrte-Real N, Ruivo P, Oliveira T. Leveraging internet of things and big data analytics initiatives in European and American firms: Is data quality a way to extract business value? Information Management. 2020;**57**(1):103141

[22] Andronie M, Lăzăroiu G, Iatagan M, Hurloiu I, Dijmărescu I. Sustainable cyber-physical production systems in big data-driven smart urban economy: A systematic literature review. Sustainability. 2021;**13**(2):751

[23] Akter S, Gunasekaran A, Wamba SF, Babu MM, Hani U. Reshaping competitive advantages with analytics capabilities in service systems. Technological Forecasting and Social Change. 2020;**159**:120180

[24] Ashrafi A, Ravasan AZ, Trkman P, Afshari S. The role of business analytics capabilities in bolstering firms' agility and performance. International Journal of Information Management. 2019;**47**:1-15

[25] Mangla SK, Raut R, Narwane VS, Zhang Z. Mediating effect of big data analytics on project performance of small and medium enterprises. Journal of Enterprise Information Management. 2020;**34**(1):168

[26] Chen Y, Lin Z. Business intelligence capabilities and firm performance: A study in China. International Journal of Information Management. 2021;**57**:102232

[27] Yalcin AS, Kilic HS, Delen D. The use of multi-criteria decision-making methods in business analytics: A comprehensive literature review. Technological Forecasting and Social Change. 2022;**174**:121193

[28] Hassani A, Mosconi E. Social media analytics, competitive intelligence, and dynamic capabilities in manufacturing SMEs. Technological Forecasting and Social Change. 2022;**175**:121416

[29] Zollo M, Winter SG. Deliberate learning and the evolution of dynamic capabilities. Organization Science. 2002;**13**:339-351. DOI: 10.1287/orsc.13.3.339.2780

[30] Kunath M, Winkler H. Usability of information systems to support decision making in the order management process. Procedia Cirp. 2019;**81**:322-327

[31] Al Halbusi H, Klobas JE, Ramayah T. Green core competence and firm performance in a post-conflict country, Iraq. Business Strategy and the Environment. 2022;**2022**:1-13. DOI: 10.1002/bse.3265

[32] Turban E, Aronson JE. Decision Support Systems and Intelligent Systems. 6th ed. New Jersey: Prentice Hall; 2001

[33] Foley É, Guillemette M. What is business intelligence? International Journal of Business Intelligence Research (IJBIR). 2010;**1**(4):1-28

[34] Niño HAC, Niño JPC, Ortega R. Business intelligence governance framework in a university: Universidad de la costa case study. International Journal of Information Management. 2020;**50**:405-412

[35] Kahaner L. Competitive Intelligence-How to Gather, Analyse, and Use Information to Move Your Business to the Top. 7 th ed. New York: Touchstone; 1996

[36] Davenport TH, Prusak L. Information Ecology: Mastering the Information and Knowledge Environment. Oxford: Oxford University Press Inc; 1997

[37] Abdelfattah F, Al Halbusi H, Al-Brwani RM. Influence of self-perceived creativity and social media use in predicting E-entrepreneurial intention. International Journal of Innovation Studies. 2022;**6**(3):119-127

[38] Robertson J, Caruana A, Ferreira C. Innovation performance: The effect of knowledge-based dynamic capabilities in cross-country innovation ecosystems. International Business Review. 2021;**2021**:101866

[39] Zahra SA, George G. The net-enabled business innovation cycle and the evolution of dynamic capabilities. Information Systems Research. 2002;**13**:147-150. DOI: 10.1287/isre.13.2.147.90

[40] Garcia AE. Inteligência competitiva: considerações sobre a prática no ambiente empresarial brasileiro. Revista Inteligência Competitiva. 2018;**8**(1):127-168

[41] Trieu V-H et al. Applying and extending the theory of effective use in a business intelligence context. MIS Quarterly. 2022;**46**(1):645-678

[42] Hassani A. Déterminants de l'intelligence compétitive et son rôle médiateur dans la relation entre la turbulence de l'environnement et la performance des PMEs. Québec: Université de Sherbrooke; 2020

[43] Eisenhardt KM, Martin J. A: Dynamic capabilities: What are they? Strategic Management Journal. 2000;**21**(10-11):1105-1121

[44] Alsaad A et al. Linking business intelligence with the performance of new service products: Insight from a dynamic capabilities perspective. Journal of Innovation & Knowledge. 2022;7(4):100262

[45] Teece D. Dynamic capabilities: Routines versus entrepreneurial action. Journal Of Management Studies. 2012;**49**(8):1395-1401

[46] Broccardo L, Truant E, Dana L-P. The interlink between digitalization, sustainability, and performance: An Italian context. Journal of Business Research. 2023;**158**:113621

[47] Matarazzo M, Penco L, Profumo G, Quaglia R. Digital transformation and customer value creation in made in Italy SMEs: A dynamic capabilities perspective. Journal of Business Research. 2021;**123**:642-656

[48] Kim G, Shin B, Kim KK, Lee H. IT capabilities, process-oriented dynamic capabilities, and firm financial performance. Journal of the Association for Information Systems. 2011;**12**(7):487

[49] Acosta-Prado JC, Campos E, Longo-Somoza M. Technological capability and development of intellectual capital on the new technology-based firms. Cuadernos de Administración. 2014;**27**(48):11-39

[50] Conboy K, Mikalef P, Dennehy D, Krogstie J. Using business analytics to enhance dynamic capabilities in operations research: A case analysis and research agenda. European Journal of Operational Research. 2020;**281**(3):656-672

[51] Mikalef P, Krogstie J, Pappas I, Pavlou P. Exploring the relationship between big data analytics capability and competitive performance: The mediating roles of dynamic and operational capabilities. Information Management. 2020;**57**(2):103169

[52] Shamim S, Zeng J, Shariq S, Khan Z. Role of big data management in enhancing big data decision-making capability and quality among Chinese firms: A dynamic capabilities view. Information Management. 2019;**56**(6):103135

[53] Goerzig D, Bauernhansl T. Enterprise architectures for the digital transformation in small and medium-sized enterprises. Procedia CIRP. 2018;**67**:540-545

[54] Chirumalla K. Building digitally-enabled process innovation in the process industries: A dynamic capabilities approach. Technovation. 2021;**105**:102256

[55] Linde L, Sjödin D, Parida V, Wincent J. Dynamic capabilities for ecosystem orchestration A capability-based framework for smart city innovation initiatives. Technological Forecasting and Social Change. 2021;**166**:120614

[56] Bianchi G, Testa F, Tessitore S, Iraldo F. How to embed environmental sustainability: The role of dynamic capabilities and managerial approaches in a life cycle management perspective. Business Strategy and the Environment. 2022;**31**(1):312-325

[57] Singh SK, Del Giudice M, Chiappetta Jabbour CJ, Latan H, Sohal A. Stakeholder pressure, green innovation, and performance in small and medium-sized enterprises: The role of green dynamic capabilities. Business Strategy and the Environment. 2022;**31**(1):500-514

[58] Jafari-Sadeghi V, Mahdiraji H, Busso D, Yahiaoui D. Towards agility in international high-tech SMEs: Exploring key drivers and main outcomes of dynamic capabilities. Technological Forecasting and Social Change. 2022;**174**:121272

[59] Mousavi S, Bossink B, van Vliet M. Dynamic capabilities and organizational routines for managing innovation towards sustainability. Journal of Cleaner Production. 2018;**203**:224-239

[60] Slater SF, Mohr J, Sengupta S. Radical product innovation capability: Literature review, synthesis, and illustrative research propositions. Journal of Product Innovation Management. 2014;**31**(3):552-566

[61] Ghobakhloo M, Iranmanesh M, Grybauskas A, Vilkas M, Petraitė M. Industry 4.0, innovation, and sustainable

development: A systematic review and a roadmap to sustainable innovation. Business Strategy and the Environment. 2021;**30**(8):4237-4257

[62] Mikalef P, van de Wetering R, Krogstie J. Building dynamic capabilities by leveraging big data analytics: The role of organizational inertia. Information Management. 2021;**58**(6):103412

[63] Jafari-Sadeghi V, Mahdiraji HA, Bresciani S, Pellicelli A. Context-specific micro-foundations and successful SME internationalisation in emerging markets: A mixed-method analysis of managerial resources and dynamic capabilities. Journal of Business Research. 2021;**134**:352-364

[64] Bağış M, Kryeziu L, Akbaba Y, Ramadani V, Karagüzel ES, Krasniqi BA. The micro-foundations of a dynamic technological capability in the automotive industry. Technology in Society. 2022;**70**:102060

[65] Teece D. Explicating dynamic capabilities: The nature and microfoundations of (sustainable) enterprise performance. Strategic Management Journal. 2007;**28**(13):1319-1350

[66] Munten P, Vanhamme J, Maon F, Swaen V, Lindgreen A. Addressing tensions in coopetition for sustainable innovation: Insights from the automotive industry. Journal of Business Research. 2021;**136**:10-20

[67] Hermundsdottir F, Aspelund A. Sustainability innovations and firm competitiveness: A review. Journal of Cleaner Production. 2021;**280**:124715

[68] Le T, Ikram M. Do sustainability innovation and firm competitiveness help improve firm performance? Evidence from the SME sector in Vietnam. Sustainable Production and Consumption. 2022;**29**:588-599

[69] Fernandes CI, Veiga P, Ferreira JJ, Hughes M. Green growth versus economic growth: Do sustainable technology transfer and innovations lead to an imperfect choice? Business Strategy and the Environment. 2021;**30**(4):2021-2037

[70] Castellano R, Punzo G, Scandurra G, Thomas A. Exploring antecedents of innovations for small-and medium-sized enterprises' environmental sustainability: An interpretative framework. Business Strategy and the Environment. 2022;**2022**

[71] Du S, Bstieler L, Yalcinkaya G. Sustainability-focused innovation in the business-to-business context: Antecedents and managerial implications. Journal of Business Research. 2022;**138**:117-129

[72] Rauter R, Globocnik D, Perl-Vorbach E, Baumgartner R. Open innovation and its effects on economic and sustainability innovation performance. Journal of Innovation and Knowledge. 2019;**4**(4):226-233

[73] Silvestre BS, Ţîrcă D. Innovations for sustainable development: Moving toward a sustainable future. Journal of Cleaner Production. 2019;**208**:325-332

[74] De Luca AI, Falcone G, Stillitano T, Iofrida N, Strano A, Gulisano G. Evaluation of sustainable innovations in olive growing systems: A life cycle sustainability assessment case study in southern Italy. Journal of Cleaner Production. 2018;**171**:1187-1202

[75] Inigo EA, Albareda L. Sustainability oriented innovation dynamics: Levels of dynamic capabilities and their path-dependent and self-reinforcing logics.

Technological Forecasting and Social Change. 2019;**139**:334-351

[76] Teece D. The foundations of enterprise performance: Dynamic and ordinary capabilities in an (economic) theory of firms. The Academy of Management Perspectives. 2014;**28**(4):328-352

[77] Cillo V, Petruzzelli A, Ardito L, Del Giudice M. Understanding sustainable innovation: A systematic literature review. Corporate Social Responsibility and Environmental Management. 2019;**26**(5):1012-1025

[78] Nylund P, Brem A, Agarwal N. Innovation ecosystems for meeting sustainable development goals: The evolving roles of multinational enterprises. Journal of Cleaner Production. 2021;**281**:125329

[79] Mousavi S, Bossink B, van Vliet M. Microfoundations of companies' dynamic capabilities for environmentally sustainable innovation: Case study insights from high-tech innovation in science-based companies. Business Strategy and the Environment. 2019;**28**(2):366-387

[80] Díaz-Chao Á, Ficapal-Cusí P, Torrent-Sellens J. Environmental assets, industry 4.0 technologies and firm performance in Spain: A dynamic capabilities path to reward sustainability. Journal of Cleaner Production. 2021;**281**:125264

[81] McKelvie A, Davidsson P. From resource base to dynamic capabilities: An investigation of new firms. British Journal of Management. 2009;**20**:S63-S80

[82] Mikalef P, Boura M, Lekakos G, Krogstie J. Big data analytics capabilities and innovation: The mediating role of dynamic capabilities and moderating effect of the environment. British Journal of Management. 2018;**30**(2):272-298. DOI: 10.1111/1467-8551.12343

[83] Sun Z, Sun L, Strang K. Big data analytics services for enhancing business intelligence. The Journal of Computer Information Systems. 2018;**58**(2):162-169

[84] Song M, Tao W, Shen Z. Improving high-quality development with environmental regulation and industrial structure in China. Journal of Cleaner Production. 2022;**366**:132997

[85] Rodrigo L, Ortiz-Marcos I, Palacios M, Romero J. Success of organisations developing digital social innovation: Analysis of motivational key drivers. Journal of Business Research. 2022;**144**:854-862

Chapter 3

Circular Systems Design: Seeking Outgrowth Based on Disruption

Ana Espada

Abstract

Innovative design has promoted the economic valorization of new ideas adopted by major companies and industrial groups. Nowadays, however, designers should instead participate in the development of a new conceptualization of modern society, based on user demands, environmental demands, and business transition for circular business models. Today's business models focus on sales, while cost reduction and the integration of more extended use or the reuse of products are not the drivers of the business. It is necessary to embrace a new mindset and generate value differently. The circular economy principles suggest the reevaluation of the current business models in order to transform circular strategies into competitive advantages, which determine the company's resilience and transform uncertainty into successful revenue models totally future-proof and innovative. In sum, circular systems design is assumed as a catalyst that promotes the transition from linear to circular business models, moving away from *take-make-dispose* and installing a more regenerative and circular economy.

Keywords: circular economy, business models, resilience, regenerative, outgrowth

1. Introduction

What is the circular economy? This is a frequently asked question. Is it a model analysis tool, a process framework, or an innovative way of defining public policy? The Circular Economy is a set of strategies that requires evaluating and developing new business models to transform circular strategies into competitive advantages, business resilience, and successful revenue models, within the limits of planet Earth. Using fewer natural resources and pursuing near-to-zero waste targets.

It is clear that sustainable development cannot be regarded merely as an environmental statement to the extent that economic and social issues are closely related. A change of mentalities is needed, basically in what concerns the consumption patterns that are implied in what is still today understood as the quality of life, if sustainability is to be attained.

Sustainability is necessarily subjective because it reflects human value — the relative importance stakeholders assign to the activity to be sustained, to the perceived benefits of that activity, and to other values "traded-off" to sustain the activity in question [1]. Additionally, due to the fact that sustainability is a long-term issue and the effects of non-sustainable behavior are often delayed in time, companies tend to focus their effort on short-term issues and avoid problems that are not imminent.

However, many companies are becoming increasingly conscious of the need to change their practices.

In fact, the environmental strategies of companies have been evolving over time. The first strategies to be introduced were of a compliant nature, that is. strictly related to environmental regulation and pollution control, and were therefore process-oriented. In order to assess compliance, these strategies make use of tools such as energy and environmental audits. Improved strategies arise with extended environmental consciousness and product responsibility, introducing life-cycle thinking.

The focus of these strategies is on products/services and on the minimization of the environmental impact throughout their life cycle, that is. from the extraction of material to final product disposal, passing the use stage. Life cycle assessment (LCA) is an assessment tool for the environmental performance of the product or service that accounts for all the relevant flows of energy and materials [2].

Design for sustainability emerges in this strategic context as a life-cycle thinking design approach in which the design goals are those of minimizing the consumption of resources, minimizing emissions, and facilitating the disposal of the product at its end-of-life, ideally with good prospects for reuse and recycling. Life cycle assessment is the preferential tool for assisting the design of the sustainability process. Finally, it is necessary to mention that the most recent and holistic environmental strategies are those based on industrial ecology. These strategies are aimed at closing loops in industrial ecosystems, namely by promoting the exchange of waste across industrial sectors and energy cascading utilization and are therefore system-oriented.

2. From take-make-dispose toward a more regenerative and circular economy

Circular value creation is recommendations at a business model level that suggest the use of one or more strategies to close, slow, or narrow resource loops accordingly to circular economy principles [3]. Circular systems design is assumed for this research purpose, as a catalyst that promotes the transition from linear to circular business models, moving away from take-make-dispose and installing a more regenerative and circular economy.

From the business point of view (economical vector of sustainability), the circular business models are being invoked, but as yet they are not widely practiced. Therefore, it is fundamental to look at the considerations of circular economy principles, which should be integrated into an early stage of the design process and understand how it impacts the value chain and the life cycle of the product and services.

2.1 Narrow, slow, and close loops in the role of design

Nowadays, more and more designers, citizens, businesses, and governments are showing a growing concern for environmental pressures related to the scarcity of global resources due to human activities and the social and environmental impacts of a consumer society. The current economies and their systems of production and consumption are stressing and damaging the Earth's natural systems. Huge amounts of raw materials and energy are used to create billions of products in order to sustain people's quality of life and consumer habits. At the same time, large volumes of waste are sent into the atmosphere, water, land, and ecosystems, which are vital to human existence.

There is a correlation between wealth and pollution and with current technological developments and the multidisciplinary approach to design, an effort must be made to provide product and service solutions that enable the user's convenience while preserving the environment. The underlying problem lies in the current linear economies that make abundant use of raw materials and natural resources, consume energy, and waste large amounts of material, which ends up as waste. This is immediately followed by new extractions of virgin material with high financial, economic, and social costs.

Circular strategies aim to keep the value of resources (**Figure 1**) and products at their highest value for as long as possible and to extend their lifetime for a prolonged period of time. These circular strategies aim to "Narrow," "Slow," and "Close" product resource flows [4].

In order to retain the value of the products and resources for as long as possible, it is necessary to create products and services that have a long-life span, but moreover, designers are expected to ensure that end users will use these products for a long time and eventually repair them.

The narrowing loops strategy reduces the amount of material per product or service, currently, in the linear economy approach. As the motivation of the companies is cost reduction, narrowing loops are already applied as resource efficiency strategies. From the point of view of design, it can be related, for example, to weight reduction or shape flexibility.

The limitation of this design strategy is that it does not necessarily contemplate the end-of-life consequences, recycling, collecting, or dismantling strategies [4]. In fact, in the current linear economy, even the products produced very efficiently and according to the narrowing strategies are thrown away after a single use.

Narrowing loops can be achieved by using fewer resources in the products, such as lean manufacturing activities, which constantly optimize the efficiency of production processes. This can also be achieved through the reduction of the weight in the automotive industry, optimizing in the production phase through the materials and processes and during the use phase by the reduction of fuel consumption. An interesting business model innovation of narrowing loops are, in fact, the combination with other strategies, for example, moving from ownership of a car to usage of a car that provides a mobility service [5].

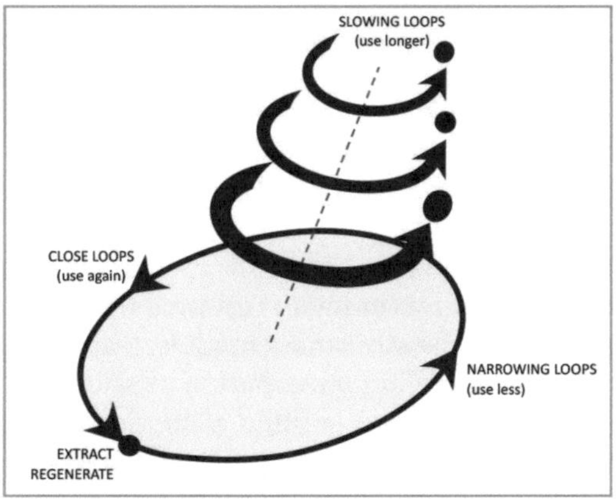

Figure 1.
Effects of the circular strategies into the usage phase.

The challenge that designers face to narrow the loops, is to make sure the product and services are developed to increase their durability. This can, however, increase the amount of materials required for production, so there needs to be a trade-off between durability and resource efficiency in production [4].

An LCA can help designers take the right decisions and predict different scenarios before considering the final design solution. For example, designing products that are easy to repair, maintain, upgrade, refurbish, and remanufacture; using modularity platforms dismantling readiness or single-layer materials may be some of the strategies where the use of more resources in production can be offset by the longer use cycle of the product [6].

The slowing loops strategy supports continuous reuse over time, and it involves innovation at the business model and value chain levels. Through the design of long-life goods, product-life extension, and service loops for repair and remanufacturing, it is possible to slow down the resources used by intensifying or expanding their use [4].

TU Delft experimented with a business model innovation aiming to slow consumption, giving customers an incentive to reduce the impact of home appliances. Consumers pay per wash rather than buy a washing machine. High-quality washing machines last longer and are built to be reused and recycled. The user is encouraged to do less and to wash at a lower temperature, by paying when they use if wash at high temperatures [4]. Another example is the Patagonia advertisement in the New York Times: "Don't buy this jacket" trying to create awareness for "slow consumption."

Considering the narrowing, the slowing and the closing of the resource's loops, the slowing strategy is the most difficult circular strategy to implement. Due to the need for several changes in the design, in the manufacturing processes and in the use phase, which represents an expressive level of uncertainty and risk for business. Nevertheless, it is also the most important strategy because it decreases the number of resources in the loop and consequently the number of waste to process and recycle. The recuperation of these resources to remanufacture or reintegrate in a new manufacturing cycle also reduces the dependence on raw materials (e.g. mining and fuel resources).

The closing loops strategy after several cycles of use is the concept introduced by Braungart and McDonough in cradle to cradle [7]. The most relevant design constraint is the use of single-layer materials since non-mixed or blended materials significantly simplify the recycling process. Design strategies of disassembly and reassembly will be instrumental in closing the loops.

In the industry, plastic, paper, and metal recycling rates are already quite significant. Recycling makes it possible to reduce the amount of waste that goes to landfills (or is dumped in the sea) and reduces the extraction of exhaustible resources. However, designers play an important role in the narrowing strategy, because, if value chains and business models analysis become part of the design process from an early stage, the products and services do not become "waste" in the first place and are instead recovered or recycled [5].

It is important to note that the transition from a linear economy to a circular economy is much broader than intervening in resource flows. This evolution will have to be supported by new policies, new business models, transformations in human behavior, and the development and implementation of strategies for the circular design of products and services in order to build a circular society.

Waste-free design, accordingly to circular principles, can help ensure that we secure enough resources for our societies to develop. This need to combine environmental, social, and economic vectors of sustainability may be considered from different perspectives, but the literature shows some common grounds.

Design for circularity requires planning for the entire life cycle of a product and service and its environmental and social effects. This requires that tools such as LCA, as mentioned above, should be an integral part of the design project. The design constraints should be established to ensure that [8]:

- future public health and safety are not compromised,
- the environment and resources are not subject to physical and chemical deterioration,
- the after use of the site is beneficial and sustainable in the long term,
- any adverse socioeconomic impacts are minimized, and.
- socio-economic benefits are maximized.

3. Why should companies seek out growth based on disruption?

Today's world lives beyond large changes compelled by socio-environmental drivers and influences all activity sectors, especially people's everyday lives. In this exploratory essay, we seek to address why businesses can seek outgrowth based on the disruption of their business model, exploring the design of circular systems.

To initiate the process of companies becoming available to transform their business models considerably, it would be advisable for manufacturers to formalize several strategic partnerships and diversify the existing supply chain.

Independently of the stakeholder activity with whom the manufacturer establishes the partnership, the nature of the partnership can profoundly influence the design strategy (and vice-versa).

Today's world lives beyond large changes compelled by socio-environmental drivers and influences all activity sectors, especially people's everyday lives. In this introductory work, we seek to address how businesses can seek outgrowth based on the disruption of their business model, exploring circular systems design and strategies.

Circular thinking in an early stage of the design process produces business model recommendations that can encourage innovation. Nevertheless, to initiate the transition process from a linear to a circular economy, it is required to ensure that the companies become available to transform their business models considerably, it would be advisable to formalize several strategic partnerships and diversify the existing supply chain.

Independently of the stakeholder activity with whom the company establishes the partnership, the nature of the partnership can profoundly influence the design strategy (and vice-versa).

According to Professor Clayton Christensen, from Harvard Business School, [9] the strategy to follow is disruptive innovation. Companies can become more competitive with disruptive innovations that either create opportunities in new markets or take over the worst customers from a well-established player. Christensen's [10] research overwhelmingly suggests that companies should seek outgrowth based on disruption (**Figure 2**).

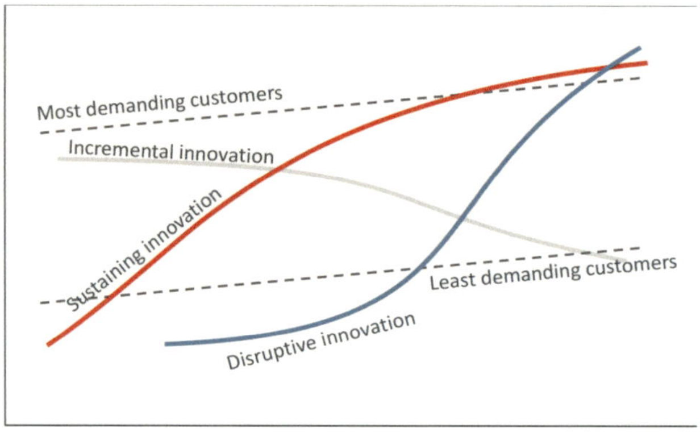

Figure 2.
Seeking growth based on disruption. Source: adapted from Kylliäinen [11].

3.1 Implement disruptive innovation

Large companies stay focused on more profitable customers and overserve adding marketing arguments and features that push the market and do not necessarily answer to a need manifested by the user. The disruptive design improves the products and services to answer the requirements of more stockholders. According to Christensen [9], disruptive innovation takes a share of the market and promotes other companies to react by launching their own disruptive innovation (e.g. CREST 3d whitestrips from P&G which is a cheap, DIY alternative to an expensive dental service).

3.1.1 Develop new value networks: Participative users change social behavior

In the *linear economy*, sustaining innovation, instead of creating new value networks, improves and extends existing ones, satisfying users' needs or generating needs for the user. The circular system's designers, at the beginning of the design process, ask "What is the end user's need?" And by the users, they are referring to all the stakeholders of the value chain.

Design performance of sustaining innovation creates value on existing products, which is typically what currently companies are doing: narrowing loops — reducing the amount of materials needed per product or service; resource efficiency; or doing more with less, which is also an opportunity to save costs. In the best-case scenario, companies perform a life cycle assessment (LCA) to understand the impacts of the materials their products have on the environment and economically (usually associated with recycling fees) — the *recycling economy*.

In the circular economy, disruptive innovation, circular systems designers must ask "How can the stakeholders be engaged and encouraged to participate from an early stage of the design process?". This change in the approach to the design process will promote different dynamics, synergies between sectors and a shift of power in the marketplaces. These happened due to the design approach being based on exploring experimentation in user behavior, stakeholders' requirements, and policy constraints.

Design for a circular economy considers what happens with the product after it has been used and before it goes for recycling (closing the loop). "Can the product be reused or remanufactured, or at least some of its parts?", "Can any of the functions offered by the product be converted into services?" — The answer to this questions depends immensely on the user's willingness and availability to participate as an active actor in the value chain. Although the current design recommendation refers to the creation of value networks at several levels of the product chain, such as at a technological level (e.g. IoT, big data, AI), logistics, R&D, and among others, the user involvement is crucial to; on the one hand, guarantee sales volumes but mainly for slowing and closing loops of material or resources.

In the circular economy, the design effort focuses on retaining the value of products and materials for as long as possible, as opposed to the current linear and recycling economy, where many efficiently manufactured products are thrown away after only being used once or at least its life span could be extended several times.

3.1.2 Narrowing loops combining design and innovation strategies

According to Donald Norman's definition [12], the main ambition of emotional design is to provoke emotions through products and services, improving the user experience. Designers focus on the emotions that can arise from the interaction of a product, and he classifies it into three categories: visceral (related to appearances), behavioral (pleasure and effectiveness of use), and reflective (rationalization and intellectualization of a product).

Narrowing loops means that circular systems designers are requested to develop concepts that consider changing users' behavior and are requested to develop products that increase the desire to keep them for longer. Today's emotional design suggestions are extended to induce users to repair, maintain, upgrade/restyle, refurbish, and remanufacture, in order to extend the use cycle of the products, thereby narrowing loops combining design and innovation strategies.

When using incremental and sustaining innovation strategies, the designed products aim to perform better than the previous generation or competition, for example, by reducing weaknesses, optimizing manufacturing processes, or transport-optimized stacking.

Using a disruptive innovation design strategy, the new product can have improved functionalities and be more profitable than the previous solutions or it targets more high-profit customers. However, it might lead to lower volumes and thus higher absolute profits. Circular systems design can make that happen if it uses a systematic approach from an early stage in the design process: Planning surrounding services and reuse, remanufacturing loops, and creating maintenance or data managing services attached to the product itself - design for dematerialization and resource reduction/ substitution.

3.1.3 Build design concept on volumes and profits arguments

As is the case in the adoption of other innovative processes, it is likely that designers will face some difficulties persuading customers or partners to implement circular and disruptive innovations. It is required to build the design concepts in a way that reduces the uncertainty inherent to any innovation. Arguments, such as volumes and profits, are critical to drive circular design or to attract new partners for a new value chain when all the stakeholders expect slow growth, but with fast profitability.

Nevertheless, volumes and profits should be considered as engagement arguments to assess risk and resistance to innovation. The three key elements that any circular business model should ideally have, and that consequently shape the design process are oriented toward value creation: i) *circular value creation*, ii) to make use of *value propositions that enable circularity*, iii) and to be *surrounded by circular value network*. We will discuss this in more detail in the next section.

Any manager of a new and growing company seeks a rapid increase in sales volumes, and circular systems designers are sure to be persuaded to make this happen. Nevertheless, it is unlikely that disruptive business achieves growth very fast. But well-established markets and circular systems design customers (manufacturers and other supply chain stakeholders) are not interested in the strengths of disruptive innovation.

The majority of the stakeholders resists innovative design solutions and will mostly focus on the weaknesses, which can drive the circular design to fail. It is important to point out that keeping the core business of the company growing healthily will make it easier for the management to wait for the (disruptive) circular business to build commercial mass slowly. In other words, the business model transition will probably be delayed and ideally planned in several stages of 3, 7, and 10 (or more) years pilot phases. Circular systems designers will share the role of facilitator with key representatives of each stakeholder, discussing innovative and sustainable matters at both technology and management levels, to orchestrate systemic change in a flexible and adaptable innovative way. And, therefore, influence information flow and risk assessment metrics throughout project development by considering alternatives and thinking beyond obvious solutions associated with the linear and/or recycling mindset.

This will also be reflected in the placement of the circular system design interventions, within the planning and project management of the transition process, which again differentiates the design thinking and the circular systems design approach.

Design thinking (eg: "double diamond" process model) and exploring experimentation are often treated as the starting point (or seed) of the design process, and innovation, for desirable societal or economical transformations. While a circular system design approach may become more demanding since it implies a mindset shift that necessarily depends on top-down recommendations from a strategic level and the involvement of internal team members responsible for the training, facilitating the unblocking along the transition period.

4. From volumes and profits to value and impact measurement

Nowadays, business models focus on sales, while cost reduction and the integration of more extended use or the reuse of products are not the drivers of business [13]. It is necessary to embrace a new mindset and generate value differently. (repeated from the abstract) It is possible to operate commercially but not oriented toward maximizing profits but toward creating value for the ecosystem and society. It will require a high commitment to reduce negative externalities and create positive externalities (especially in R&D and training and education).

As previously mentioned, there are three key components that any circular business model should ideally have. These components are:

- to engage in a preliminary form of circular value creation. To include one or more ways to close, slow, or narrow resource loops;

- to make use of value propositions that enable circularity. This depends on the needs and motivations of the final users:

- Circular branding strategy, adequate to a more informed and demanding final user, environmentally sensitive,

- Premium brand strategy, products that last a lifetime,

- Product-service strategy, where a company owns and delivers the product as a service instead of selling it,

- Reducing costs to the final user, when a cheaper product or service is offered, providing a platform to share underutilized capacity, or eliminating product stocks by production on demand.

- to be surrounded by a circular value network, when all stages of a product life cycle are connected in a way assuring that the product and its resources are maintained inside the economy. Value networks can be established for several purposes:

- A deposit refund scheme improves the return of goods to the producer,

- Online platforms can be used to manage the movement of goods in a network,

- Setting up a value network at a local scale can help avoid the loss of resources in complex global value chains.

These three values reduce the uncertainty approaching circularity accordingly to design strategies and support the communication between the team members.

4.1 Value creation and impact assessment: the design role

Circular design is a philosophy extensively used nowadays and widely acknowledged as the development paradigm still to be followed. Circular Design cannot be regarded just as an environmental statement to the extent that closely related are economic and social issues.

A change of mindset and behavior is fundamental. In what concerns the consumption patterns that are implied in what is still today understood as a quality of life, if circularity is to be attained [14].

For generators of design constraints, it is the user that is the ultimate carrier of uncertainty, and the user can delay the adoption of innovations carried to the market within the circular economy. James Woudhuysen [15] discusses that it is needed to distinguish between the user's subjective perception of change before it becomes a reality and its implementation.

Nevertheless, the success of design solutions breakthroughs does not directly depend on users' perceptions of change, but on its acceptance when it is massively distributed. On the other hand, inciting Lord Keynes in Cities for a Small Planet, Richard Rogers [16] brings up the argument that it is much easier to introduce a radically new idea, rather than to exempt from an old one.

This argument is, however, sometimes counteracted by that in which it is believed that users accept new ideas but need some continuity to push them softly to change. This way, radical or disruptive discontinuity makes things difficult or impossible to implement. Whatever the prevalent idea is, and from a design point of view, this resistance to change creates a momentum to identify the future windows of opportunities and to simulate usability contexts that may shed some light on the reaction to a given innovation — the circular approach at a product, value proposition, or at business model levels.

Design for circularity is necessarily subjective because it reflects human value — the relative importance stakeholders assign to the activity to be sustained— to the perceived benefits of that activity, and to other values "traded-off" to sustain the activity in question [1]. Additionally, the fact that circular economy is a long-term issue and that the effects of noncircular behavior are often delayed in time, companies tend to focus their effort on near-term issues and avoid problems that are not imminent. However, many companies are becoming increasingly conscious of the need to change their practices.

In fact, the environmental strategies of companies have been evolving. The first strategies to be introduced were of a compliance nature, that is. strictly related to environmental regulation and pollution control, and were therefore process-oriented. To assess compliance, these strategies make use of tools such as energy and environmental audits. Improved strategies arise with extended environmental consciousness and product responsibility, introducing lifecycle thinking.

The focus of these strategies is on products/services and the minimization of the environmental impact throughout their lifecycle, that is. from material extraction to final product disposal, passing the use stage. LCA is an assessment tool of the environmental performance of the product or service that accounts for all the relevant flows of energy and materials [2].

Design for sustainability emerges in this strategic context as a lifecycle thinking design approach in which the design goals are those of minimizing the consumption of resources, decarbonization, and facilitating the disposal of the product at its end-of-life, ideally with excellent prospects for reuse and recycle.

Finally, it is necessary to mention that the most recent and holistic environmental strategies are those based on industrial ecology. These strategies are aimed at closing loops in industrial ecosystems, namely by promoting the exchange of wastes across industrial sectors and energy cascading utilization and are therefore system-oriented.

When designing for sustainability, a large number of actors may be involved in the process, and that will imply a mutual understanding of problems and the identification of common interests and possible synergies, the mutual exploration of different solutions and finally, defining and fine-tuning a common objective. In the process, opportunities for innovating, while delivering more environmentally responsible products, are most likely to occur.

4.2 Circular design implementation strategies

Design, among other fields, is feeling pressure to adapt to goal on the European Green Deal. It aims climate neutrality by 2050 and includes [17–19] zero pollution, affordable and secure energy, smarter transport, and high-quality food. It provides a roadmap with actions that are relevant to the product value chain and its supply chain:

User centered design strategies	Manufacturing centered design strategies	Industrial synergies design strategies
Design for DURABILITY Products that succeed in meeting the consumer's requirements (functionality, esthetic...) for long time. **EMOTIONAL Design** Products that strives to create an emotional attachment for the user. Users want to keep using longer.	**Design for for REPAIR** Correct faults to prolong product life.	**Waste-free Design for END-OF-LIFE RECYCLING** Design the products to be transformed in reusable materials for unknown products.
	Design for for SHARE Use, occupy, or enjoy a product jointly with another or others.	**Waste-free Design for WASTE VALORIZATION** Design allows valorization of industrial waste in packaging, other component or industrial sector.
	Design for for REUSE Use again or several times the product with the same function.	
Design for DEMATERIALIZATION Design that meets the user needs using no material or significatively less materials.	**Design for REMANUFACTURING** Rebuild the product with original specifications, using reused, repaired and new parts.	**Waste-free Design for REUSE OF PARTS** Design products which parts can be functional in other products or aftermarket parts.
	Design for REFURBISHMENT Renovation/restyling to prolong the product life.	
	Design for DISMANTLING Take a product apart to facilitate reuse/repair/recycling parts.	
	Design for MATERIAL RECOVERY Valorization of production waste in the same production.	
	Design with SECONDARY MATERIAL Use of materials recycled from unknown companies.	
	Design with TAKE-BACK MATERIAL Use in the same product, materials collected from the user	

Table 1.
Design strategies to increase product circularity.

- to boost the efficient use of resources by moving to a clean, circular economy;
- to restore biodiversity and cut pollution.

Over the last few years, the focus has been in the effort to reduce material losses and bring materials back into new material loops. European countries have been successful recovering materials from industrial residues and reintegrating them in the production process, and at the end of the product life, bringing materials back into the loop through, for example. Waste collection systems and treatment facilities. But recycling and waste management are insufficient to reach those goals. The development of tangent cycles is required in the design of circular products, to manage the products and the material in a new approach and evolve in the direction of dematerialization.

The conventional cycles refer to dismantling end-of-life products and sort them into single materials, which are used as raw materials for new products. The inner cycles refer to different strategies to retain value by extending the lifetime of the actual product. And only after cycle longer in the economy they return to their material basics functions.

These endurance cycles are shorter than the conventional loops and are achieved through repair, reuse, and remanufacturing design strategies (**Table 1**). Design for refurbishing or remanufacturing strategies also set up shorter loops allowing designers to create a loop back to the production stage, keeping the value and functionality of the products in circular savings for longer.

In **Table 1**, the relation between the several cycles is represented and based on this scheme; several circular business model archetypes can be explored as bringing to a design solution. Short loops, as in the design for repair strategy, can quickly return to the use phase. Slightly longer loops such as in the design for repair strategy can extend product lifetime. And the long loop either retains value in the loop for longer through the durability of the design solution (which is presumed as a basic request of circularity) or by design for reuse strategy where the same product goes back to other stakeholders of the value chain several times during its lifecycle. For example, a washing machine can be designed to be repaired or lent to optimize its life while in the" use" stage of the value chain. A water bottle, which is refilled by the user, is also a strategy to prolong the use of the product. But if the user goes to the retailer to fill the water bottle is a new loop. Reuse loops are often avoided due to the complexity of partner management and logistics, but with the digitalization of the industry, that complexity can be overcome.

5. Conclusions

Waste-free design, accordingly to circular principles, can help ensure that we secure enough resources for our society's development. This need to combine environmental, social, and economic vectors of sustainability may be considered from different perspectives, but the literature shows some common grounds.

Circular value creation is recommendations at a business model level that suggest the use of one or more strategies to close, slow, or narrow resource loops. Several strategies were identified, such as recycling, repairing, remanufacturing, and reusing.

From a social perspective, it is expected that the new retailer options will be characterized by a better environmental profile than its contemporaneous, ones in order for the same service — making goods available — to be made accessible with a smaller environmental burden.

Design solutions that drastically optimize the resources involved in the products, by simplifying the role played by manufacturers, distributors, retailers, and users, promote an increase in the number of cycles of use of the plastic product, as well as increasing the percentage of recovery for recycling.

Ultimately, from general design parameters, innovation in products has to emerge, taking into consideration human aspirations and worries, characteristics from the design process.

Author details

Ana Espada
Lisbon Uni., IST-ID, Lisbon, Portugal

*Address all correspondence to: acespada@gmail.com

References

[1] Tester JW et al. Sustainable Energy—Choosing among Options. Cambridge, Massachusetts, United States: The MIT Press; 2005. Available from: https://mitpress.mit.edu/books/sustainable-energy

[2] Ferrão PMC. Industrial ecology: A step towards sustainable development. In: Pereira MS, editor. A Portrait of State-of-the-Art Research at the Technical University of Lisbon. Netherlands: Springer; 2007. pp. 357-383. DOI: 10.1007/978-1-4020-5690-1_23

[3] Clift R. Taking Stock of Industrial Ecology. Berlin Heidelberg: Springer; 2015

[4] Bocken NM, De Pauw I, Bakker C, van der Grinten B. Product design and business model strategies for a circular economy. Journal of Industrial and Production Engineering. 2016;**33**(5):308-320

[5] Blomsma F, Brennan G. The emergence of circular economy: A new framing around prolonging resource productivity. Journal of Industrial Ecology. 2017;**21**(3):603-614. DOI: 10.1111/jiec.12603

[6] Manninen K, Koskela S, Antikainen R, Bocken N, Dahlbo H, Aminoff A. Do circular economy business models capture intended environmental value propositions? Journal of Cleaner Production. 2018;**171**:413-422. DOI: 10.1016/j.jclepro.2017.10.003

[7] McDonough W, Braungart M. Cradle to Cradle: Remaking the Way we Make Things. Heidelberg, Germany: Farrar, Straus and Giroux; 2010

[8] Gorissen L, Manshoven S, Vrancken K. Tailoring business model innovation towards grand challenges: Employment of a transition management approach for the social enterprise "re-use centers". Journal of Global Responsibility. 2014;**5**(2):289-311. DOI: 10.1108/JGR-03-2014-0012

[9] Christensen C, McDonald RM, Altman EJ, Palmer J. Disruptive innovation: Intellectual history and future paths. Academy of Management Proceedings. 2017;**2017**(1):14218. DOI: 10.5465/AMBPP.2017.14218abstract

[10] Christensen CM, Raynor ME, Anthony SD. Six Keys to Building New Markets by Unleashing Disruptive Innovation—Harvard Business School Working Knowledge. 9 Mar 2003. Available from: https://hbswk.hbs.edu/item/six-keys-to-building-new-markets-by-unleashing-disruptive-innovation

[11] Kylliäinen. Viima (17/04/2023). 2019. Available from: https://www.viima.com/blog/disruptive-innovation

[12] Norman DA, Verganti R. Incremental and radical innovation: Design research vs. technology and meaning change. Design Issues. 2013;**30**(1):78-96. DOI: 10.1162/DESI_a_00250

[13] Pardo R. A Long-Term Strategy for a European Circular Economy – Setting the Course for Success. London, United Kingdom: IEEP and Jean-Pierre Schweitzer, Product Policy and Circular Economy Office, EEB; 2018. p. 33

[14] Ellen-MacArthur-Foundation. Ellen-MacArthur-Foundation-Towards-the-Circular-Economy: Business Rationale for an Accelerated Transition-vol.1.pdf. 2015

[15] Woudhuysen J. The craze for design thinking: Roots, a critique, and toward an

alternative. 2011. Available from: https://dora.dmu.ac.uk/handle/2086/5561

[16] Rogers R. Cities for a small planet. World Heritage Review. 1996;**3**:68-77

[17] European Commission. A European Strategy for Plastics in a Circular Economy. 2018. Available from: https://eur-lex.europa.eu/legal-content/EN/TXT/HTML/?uri=CELEX:52018DC0028&from=EN

[18] Charter M. Designing for the Circular Economy. New York, United States: Routledge; 2018

[19] Coursera. Circular Economy—Sustainable Materials Management. Coursera. 2020. Available from: https://www.coursera.org/learn/circular-economy

Chapter 4

Corporate Governance in the South African Public Agencies: Implications for Oversight and Accountability Mechanisms

Noluthando Shirley Matsiliza

Abstract

Government oversight mechanisms are imperative to sustain state-owned enterprises (SOEs) in an emerging economy like South Africa. This chapter explores corporate governance challenges and opportunities and their implications for oversight mechanisms and accountability in the South African SOEs. Corporate governance (CG) can be understood as the principles, rules, and practices in which the organizational systems are governed while also balancing the interests of the organizations and that of stakeholders such as senior managers, executives, customers, stakeholders, and government. CG can be applied as a management tool that serves interests that are neither purely public nor purely private while ensuring their growth and productivity. Governments devote tremendous attention and interest to enterprise risk management since the global economic collapse (ERM). Even though SOEs adopted CG to safeguard their growth path in performance and productivity, they have been observed as yielding negative productivity that is not cushioning the economy in the right direction, while also eliciting gaps in CG and risk management of SOEs. The contents of this chapter include the conceptual and theoretical approaches to CG and challenges in applying CG in an international, African, and local context. This chapter prioritizes the implications of compliance and oversight in the South-African SOEs.

Keywords: accountability, corporate governance, corruption, risk management, state capacity and public enterprises

1. Introduction

Corporate governance (CG) is not new in South Africa. Private sector is ahead of public agencies in the application of CG principles despite the absence of a legal prescript that supports it. The South-African government mandates state-owned enterprises (SOEs) to steer the direction of development efforts of its emerging economy while using diverse oversight mechanisms and policies in public agencies [1]. Therefore, the government functions under the assumption that SOEs must direct projects that advance the country's mixed economy. The advancement of the economy through SOEs productivity is supported by a free market system globally, while the SOEs activities produce bottom-up, with effective results without the involvement of the state [2]. It can be pronounced that the SA mixed economy caters for both the private and public sectors, where the public sector goal is to support the welfare of the society. The global impact of COVID-19 and Omicron spreading affected the economy, and there is a probability that it will have a global impact on the economy in 2023 also.

This chapter argues that the systematic global and local challenges impact the South-African economy. Hence, SOEs are also affected by these challenges, and they are interconnected to socioeconomic and political environmental factors that constantly influence their decision-making. This serves as the foundation for the debate on the effectiveness of social democracy in which the interaction between the market and the state through agencies is apparent. According to Armitage, emerging economies are characterized by market-based transactions influenced by political, economic, and social factors emerging from business-dominated ownership of private investors. This situation is familiar to the South African economy that is expected to provide leverage to growing parastatals owned by the state. State-owned enterprises are emerging as agencies that are managed by a board of directors that have mixed interests. In the post-apartheid era, SOEs are anticipated to persuade economic growth and distribute real public services [3]. This chapter analyzes the application of codes of CG in SOEs, on the principles of Kings Reports, which support the notion of the state, shareholders, executive, and nonexecutive managers, clients, and communities as all guardians of accountability and good governance. This chapter also focuses mainly on the challenges in the application of corporate governance by the SOEs in South Africa.

This chapter adopted a qualitative research methodology for collecting and analyzing data. Data are mainly drawn from books, scholarly accredited journal articles, reports, policies, and legislation on CG. Despite the market's current state of development and the proper alignment of the market and the state, state-owned and publicly run businesses are a working illustration of how the government uses business principles like efficiency to offer public goods and services. The SOE in South Africa are in the spotlight of public scrutiny due to their staggering performance, especially in the energy and transport sector. The SOE's outlook is coupled with inconsistencies to achieve their mandates and goals that require them to balance their costs of operations with the production to provide services to their clients.

1.1 Research methodology and procedures

A qualitative document analysis was adopted. Qualitative research suits this chapter since it is based on the performance of SOEs as organizations with structures formed by policies and people who are observed and reported to perform in real-life situations. Brynard et al. ([4]:82) assert that the richness of document analysis lies in its nature of allowing the creation of themes from the transcribed filtered notes recorded from the documents being analyzed. This chapter adopted themes from current policy reports and articles on SOEs.

Literature was surveyed from other international and local cases that have applied CG in state entities and parastatals. Secondary data were drawn from various books, articles from accredited journals, commissioned studies reports, and government policies. The King I, II, III, and IV Reports and the OECD Network [5] Reports on CG were also sourced to understand CG. Data were first organized and filtered to exclude all the irrelevant topics. Content and discourse analyses enabled the researcher to produce themes on the gaps in the application of CG. There is an advantage of using document analysis that adds value to this study because it evaluates physical and electronic documents to interpret them. Therefore, it improves the understanding of the content and context of information generated from secondary data and delivers them. Some of the significant steps in the document analysis of this study included the following:

This study followed a procedure that is tabulated in **Table 1**, with steps sourced from the analysis of documents and policies about the performance of SOEs in

1. List of resources.	During the research planning, various sources were identified. Sources were identified based on the following reasons: 1. Medium – documents were sources including magazines, newspapers, and government bulletins. 2. Genre – genre was observed as based on politics, social issues, and political agendas. 3. Including criteria – such as news websites and section comments on local papers. 4. Parameters – parameters that indicate the date, location, demarcation of eras on administration, and range.
2. Organizing information	The researcher established two components for organizing as a set of categories and units of meaning: Sets of categories are features of the material and a unit of meaning refers to aspects you are targeting to use in your texts, such as images, phrases, and words. The researcher decided to include conceptual categories such as board ethical governance, board of directors, agency, accountability, and some category of objectives identified in the literature review.
3. Note important facts	Information was highlighted and annotated while avoiding tampering with the unique documents. Copies were filed by the researcher for future research once the study was done.
4. Ensuring authenticity	It is important to guide against biases and identify reliable sources used to aid this research; so the author observed trustworthiness before utilizing their information [4]. The researcher listed and cited copyright information, for instance, where sources are frequently provided in the documentation of authoritative sources. By validating elements like the following, one was sure a document is trustworthy: Credibility Dependability Conformability Transferability Authenticity
5. Check biases	Biases imply that there was less creativity on the side of the author/researcher. It is important to use relevant information that is not distorted and inaccurate. In this chapter, people's opinions were cited to avoid plagiarism. Even though it can be difficult to analyze data in document analysis, the author of this chapter avoided biasedness, plagiarism, and cultural bias.
6. Ask questions	Asking questions to learn more about the history of the document and how the resources might aid your study will help you undertake document analysis effectively. When evaluating material to acquire crucial details, researchers frequently ask the who, what, when, where, and why questions.
7. Evaluate and analyze	When all the above steps were done, there was a framework for approaching document analysis. Data were interpreted to produce findings that are used and discussed in this chapter.

Source: Adopted from Bowen [6].

Table 1.
Document analysis trajectory.

post-apartheid South Africa. Policy analysis was built by Taylor [7], has subsequently built over a systematic theoretical framework, and elaborates on the content and context of the literature which must be analyzed and organized into themes that relate to facts about the policy implications. Government policies and reports on policy outcomes provide information about the outcomes of policy implementation and the application of CG. Users of information must share and disseminate information on CG with credibility. Scholars in the field of management studies and others interrogated the literature and provided in-depth analysis to be learned by other scholars and users of information worldwide. It has also been noticed that information has also been questioned and validated to allow scholars to analyze information from various standpoints to allow future research.

1.2 Oversight roles of executive institutions

The term "oversight" refers to the informal and formal, strategic, vigilant, and organized examination and monitoring used by legislators to examine compliance to laws and accountability, budget requirements, and how strictly legal prescripts and the 1996 Constitution of the Republic of South Africa are followed. Legislative bodies are required by oversight to monitor the daily exercise of power by the national, provincial, and local executive branches. As part of the oversight, there is monitoring done of onsite inspections, ad hoc parliamentary and legislative inquiries, review and approval of municipal and government spending, the establishment of standing committees that cover a range of policy areas and are independent of the executive. The requirement that ministers regularly provide Parliament with information, such as annual departmental reports, and the provision of a question period for lawmakers during official proceedings are typical oversight mechanisms and techniques.

When it comes to SOEs, portfolio committees and executive institutions played a prominent role in the oversight of SOEs. Concerning the South African government, the oversight role is constitutionally arranged, among the three spheres of government. At the national level, the oversight is divided among the three powerhouses of the legislature, executive, and judicial houses.

1.3 Corporate governance conceptualization and application

The concept of "corporate governance" has been framed as the act of how organizations direct and oversee their activities. CG is applied through systems of governance with various stakeholders and members of the board with diverse interests. Various activities include the functioning of the board, the council's arrangements for effective leadership, stewardship, auditing, administration, accounting, and performance to deliver services to clients while complying with policies and procedures. Executives' and nonexecutive members' responsibilities are specified with well-rounded values and cultures supporting the systems. Globalization has influenced the way corporates rule in the world through international standards, by macrolevel, to support the allocation of the nation's savings to its most productive use. Some investments and savings are expected to be achieved and be able to fund business activities, whether through equity or debt and returns that will eventually regulate national prosperity.

Lessons can be learned from the recent US experience with Enron, WorldCom, and other failures which reminds us of systemic implications for strategic investment that may leak if sustainability is not accomplished, and business failures are adequately inescapable. Emerging economies like South Africa have a problem integrating government with business interests. The SOEs agencies and parastatals have applied CG with some reservations since there are disparities in handling business from a public and a private point of view; hence, at some point, public and private partnerships and contracts emerged.

In **Table 2**, key principles of corporate governance are highlighted. In 1994, King 1 Report was established and a few principles of CG. Later, there was a new version of the second and third reports that developed and refined the principles from the first one to the fourth report [9]. The fourth report summarized all the principles with additional ones that include more stakeholder involvement in IT governance and disclosure. The application of these principles in the governance of the SOEs implies the diverse representation of shareholders and interests from the public and private sectors. The interesting part is that there is an inclusion of ethics and other good governance principles, especially from King III to King IV. In the South African context, the inclusion of the New Public Management Principles (NPM) was made clear during the transformation of the public service and recognized the involvement of the private entities in service delivery through public and private partnerships and contrast.

1.4 Agency theory and corporate responsibility

The agency theory is fit to be aligned with CG as it is adopted to understand the relationship between the agency and the principal. In addition, the SOEs internationally and locally have adopted CG, with implications for the agency–principal relationship. Agency theory can be adopted in this study to understand the relationship between the principal and the agency. The focus of agency work in a business is how the agents protect the principal's best interests, without considering their own. The introduction of the new public management (NPM) in the South African public service implied that the government introduced new alternative ways of improving service delivery.

With the introduction of the NPM in South Africa, the government portrayed a new look at their marriage of convenience with the private sector and nongovernmental organizations. The government introduced new alternatives to improve service delivery such as public and private partnerships, management contracts, and leasing. All these new strategies were practised by integrating private interests with public interests. As absorbed by them, there was a thin line to differentiate the differences between public good and bottom-up since there was growing competition and rivalry among the SOEs and the nongovernment organizations. There was a growing conflict of interests and corruption in SOEs and resulting in nonallegiance toward the principal's best interests. Miscommunication and disagreement raised a variety of issues and strife inside government businesses.

The other interesting issue that emerges from the agency and principal relationship is that of patronage tendencies. Patronage is understood as the act of giving power to the agencies to make official bureaucratic appointments. Hollibaugh [10] notes patronage tendencies that emerge when public officials recognize certain traits such as loyalty and merits. Patronage appointees – often defined as those chosen for their campaign experience, electoral benefit, or other nonpolicy political benefits – tend to be assigned to low-priority organizations whose goals align with the president's and to positions where their influence on agency outcomes will be minimal. A case in point is

King 1	King II	King III	King IV
1. Board of directors – make up an appointment	Directors and their responsibilities	Incorporation of global trends	Recognition of committees for audit, risk, remuneration, social, and ethics
2. Determinants and disclosure of executives and nonexecutives	Accounting and auditing	Shareholders' approval of nonexecutive directors' remuneration	Effective control – mandatory rotation on audits
3. Board meeting frequency	Board meetings and ad-hoc meetings	Evaluation of the board of directors performance	Good performance-broader performance measurement is required
4. Balanced annual reporting	Integrated sustainable reporting	Integrated reporting	Transparent and meaningful reporting to stakeholders
5. Requirement for effective auditing	Internal audit	Risk-based internal audit	Internal audit
6. Risk management	Risk management	Risk management	Risk management, compliance, and assurance
7. Affirmative action programmes			Diversity management, balanced governance composition. Fair remuneration across the board.
8. Companies code of ethics			Ethical leadership and culture
9.		Alternative dispute resolution	Corporate responsibility
10.		IT governance	Technology and information
11.		Business rescue	Sustainable governance
12.		Fundamentals during mergers requisition	
13.		Global reporting on OECD guidelines on multinational companies.	Good governance
14.		Shareholders compliance	Legitimacy and shareholders' compliance
15.		UN global compact and responsible investment.	
16.		OECD guidelines, and the UK Companies Act of 2006.	

Source: Robinson et al. [8].

Table 2.
King reports on the principles of CG.

the investigation of the office of the public protector revealed malicious and corrupt tendencies between the state and the few businesses that were given contracts consistently by public officials to render government work [11].

DOI: http://dx.doi.org/10.5772/intechopen.110391

1.5 The strategic roles of SOEs in South Africa

The emergence of CG in South Africa proceeded after the infusion of the NPM principles in the South African Public Service as part of the transformation agenda. The NPM welcomed the involvement of nongovernmental and private entities to partner with the government as service providers to improve the performance of parastatals and government departments. Therefore, the public and private sectors had to find ways to work together for convenience while having diverse interests. CG emerged as a convenient approach used by both private and public organizations to manage the operations of SOEs in Southern Africa. Public organizations have implemented and climatized King's corporate governance model in the absence of a law guiding them on how to operate in South Africa.

Global and national forces, such as the technical development of international markets, increased the size and complexity of businesses, compelled them to work together more frequently, and increased the amount of capital they needed to survive and contribute to the national economy. According to Balbuena [12], most of the governments in Southern Africa have taken a similar path in the development of SOEs by privatizing some of their shares to develop their economies. In most countries like South Africa and Botswana, governments have also bailed these entities financially during their economic downswing. It is, therefore, not easy to find sustainable growth in SOEs.

To accelerate development and transformation, the government had to implement measures like privatization, which involved asking the private sector to develop the South African economy and create job opportunities. The agency theory and privatization theory are used as avenues for investment and collaboration in projects for global development and transformation.

Privatization is the process whereby the entity sells some of its stake or shares to private organizations or people who own a business. Privatization has been associated with the market economy where the bottom line and profit-making are the keys to success in boosting the economy. However, in a mixed economy like South Africa, privatization is favored by the private sector, and the public sector is aligned with the state interest of serving the general welfare. With growing globalization in the fourth Industrial Revolution (4IR), SOEs are created to support the economy by producing goods and services, and job creation. It should be noted that some stakeholders like workers' unions and other political parties contested the privatization of some of SOE, especially in the transport and energy sectors. Privatization is blamed for increased costs of production and prices of services delivered by SOEs to their clients [12]. However, it should be highlighted that SOEs are required to focus their efforts on providing goods and services to their clients and consumers, as well as saving costs and increasing profits. This chapter can classify three types of public entities listed and endorsed by Public Finance Management. The first is composed of Schedule 1 entities which include constitutional institutions such as the *Independent Electoral Commission* and *Public Protector* among others. Schedule 2 entities are comprised of Major Public Entities with greater autonomy than Schedule 3 entities. Schedule 2 entities are listed below. The subdivision of Schedule 3 entities is as follows:

- **National Public Entities** – its purpose is specialized agencies or not-for-profit organization functions such as the *Companies and Intellectual Property Commission*, the *Human Sciences Research Council*, and the *Road Accident Fund*;

- **National Government Business Enterprises** – these enterprises function as profit-seeking businesses such as the *Council for Scientific and Industrial Research, Passenger Rail Agency of South Africa* and *Rand Water*;

- **Provincial Public Entities** – these selected entities can be found in selected provinces, and they include *Gautrain Management Agency* and numerous provincial gambling and liquor boards.

- **Provincial Government Business Enterprises** – they are profit-seeking businesses controlled by the provincial government and include the *Richards Bay Industrial Development Zone* and the *East London Industrial Development Zone*.

Governments around the world have long created SOEs with several public policy objectives in mind, constructing fundamental physical infrastructure; offering necessary services such as finance, water, and energy; producing essential goods and services, resource management, market failures addressed; and other benefits for the broader society. According to Sarika [13], the SOE's existence has long been directed toward the developmental state agenda to boost the economic needs of the society by pursuing job creation and production of essential services and operations, especially in the energy and transport sectors. The agenda for development and acknowledgment of human rights motivated the government to drive SOEs toward the right path aligned to the projects and infrastructure on roads and transport toward the fulfillment of the dream for sustainable economic prosperity and economic liberation in Africa, SADC, BRICS, and SA. Therefore, the government's role in balancing political, economic, and social sectors from the 1970s and 1980s from a variety of nations suggests an average low growth is yielded in Southern Africa. This suggests that the SOE's challenges are crippling diverse projects that could improve the Southern economic development and investments. In addition, it is not a train smash to balance the government's political will and the economic goals of these SOEs and private firms for their economic prosperity.

2. Challenges of CG practices and policies

2.1 The international experience

Globally, organizations are currently operating in the environment of global financial sustainability, ecological overshoot, the climate change problem, and catastrophe that speak for themselves, for ethical governance requirements, and for compliance [14]. These aspects have been used correctly and incorrectly by various private and public institutions, individuals, businesses, governments, and other institutions. The planet's natural resources quicker than nature can replenish them, and also can be innovative and increase stakeholder expectations, open evolution, and population expansion. For the past 150 years, businesses have operated using yesterday's economic model based on two incorrect assumptions [14]. It has been assumed that in the first place, nature had endless resources, while resources are depleting, and signs are showing that human nature is a source of problematic arrangements of governance. Resource management is a challenge especially since land, water, air, coal, oil, and timber are all limited. All these resources are exploited by leaders and managers in various organizations; hence, the operation of the SOEs depends on these resources. CG as a model with required skills is suitable for running a business that accommodates both private and public entities with new demands for sustainability and ethical governance. Atinyo and Kawor [15] assessed the relationship between Corporate Governance and Financial Crisis in Ghana and attest that the major causes of the financial crisis can be linked to the failure of members of boards and management to comply with stringent CG principles and failure to identify and manage risk in various entities. The speculation on the causal link between financial bankruptcies and crises to failure to comply with CG in some entities persists throughout the world (Ong, & Djajadikerta [16]. The loosely arranged structures of governance with less-competent members of the boards that make decisions can degrade CG. As a result, the current economic systems in many countries can only work when they are a hybrid to sustain development and cushion the SOEs. By 2050, the United Nations projected that there will be an additional two billion people on the earth that will need resources. Many countries already have issues with food security and a shortage of fresh water. Given all these factors, it is obvious that no business can be done without challenges on how resources can be used or distributed, especially financial and human resources. In most countries globally, corporate entities provide support to fight the global crisis of economic meltdown due to COVID-19D 19 and other disasters. Parastatals and the SOEs have been at the forefront to support the development and economic growth in most countries. The main challenge in the operation of these entities is noncompliance and lack of accountability [17].

2.2 African experiences

In many African nations, SOEs are regarded as significant economic sectors and play a significant role in the advancement of the country through job creation, production, and service delivery. This is illustrated through access to essential services including water, energy, health, sanitation, telecommunications, and transportation and is made possible by SOEs. Small- and medium-sized businesses, which make up the majority of the private sector-led economy, rely largely on the infrastructure and services that these businesses offer to maintain their competitive position. On a regional scale, SOEs are major actors in significant cross-border infrastructure projects, which are essential to attaining what is thought to be a primary development aim and realizing regional integration aspirations. Because of their lucrative role, the public interest is mixed with business interest, and it is a bone of contention since it is a source of corruption to those managing these entities.

Besides sustainable governance, companies are acclimatizing themselves to CG by following new arrangements to manage enterprises and companies through the board of directors and a culture of principles and the interests of shareholders. Amartey et al. [18] assessed CG in Ghana and assert that there is a need for a rotation of auditing firms that assessed the application of compliance of CG in Ghana companies. Agyei-Mensah [19] also assessed CG in Ghana and argue that the absence of enforcement tools hurts the application of CG in Ghana, even though there is internal control information disclosure.

The idea of corporate citizenship is becoming more and more popular. Gurumoorthi [20] alluded to the experience and arrangement of CG in Botswana and assets that for every Botswana citizen, the government is obliged to act properly through agencies and keep others, neighbors, safe. Thus, it is anticipated that the legal entity, the corporation, operates in this capacity and honors corporate citizens. The global standard for reporting is evolving toward integrated trends on a global scale and is impacting African firms' and organizations' practices of CG (Botswana Accountancy Oversight Authority [21].

Companies must submit clear and intelligible financial reports expressing the effects of their efforts, both good and negative, socially, environmentally, and financially that affected a community. It entails a picture of the company's performance that is comprehensive and integrated in terms of both its sustainability and financial standing. Magang and Magang [22] contend that despite Botswana's low levels of compliance with international best practices, the researchers have concluded that Botswana Unified Revenue Service's (BURS's) departure from these practices has the potential to result in among other things, incompetence, corruption, bad administration, dominance, cronyism, and, in the end, a weak institution. Botswana has been excluded from international practice. Agyemang is of the view that countries' SOEs are geared toward investments depending on their capabilities.

According to CG practices, the capability of an organization can drive corporate practices and succeed in attracting capital providers based on its strength and resources. Mostly, companies and agencies can achieve great success if they can also induce capital providers to invest in businesses that can yield economic growth and benefit from their social responsibility strategy. Some of the countries like Zimbabwe have not succeeded in generating proper investment from SOEs due to their weak corporate governance that can safeguard the country's interests [23].

Josiah et al. [24] assessed the compliance of CG in Botswana and found that Botswana has not fully complied with international best practices. The case of Bostwana is not unique since they are also exposed to the mismanagement of funds, as a result, CG in the SOEs cannot safeguard their investment. The main problem is centered around the mismanagement of finances. Agyei-Mensah [19] asserts that in Botswana, the relationship between corporate governance, corruption, and forward-looking information disclosure are not stable as a result there are unstable financial governance responsibilities of the board of directors to maintain good auditing and management of financial affairs.

2.3 South African challenges

2.3.1 Understanding and compliance with regulatory measures

The South African experience is interesting since the economy has inherited the apartheid legacy of a racial society with many inequalities and a dual society where you find income disparities. The economy is strongly supported by both the public and private sectors. Even though there are no direct policies to regulate SOEs, the King I–IV Reports have been used to apply CG by private firms and the SOEs in South Africa with little success in understanding the regulatory measures as policies and the principles of corporate governance specified by the Kings Reports. The SOEs in South Africa play a strategic role to contribute to the economy, especially during the post-apartheid period when the government of national unity restructured SOEs to perform relatively better than in the past. Evidence from the 1970s, 1980s, and to the present, several SOEs in SA performed unwell relative to private firms due to the demands and standards set to them, and the environment in which they operate.

According to Thabane and Snyman-Van Deventer [25], the government of national unity in 2014 inherited some of the underperforming SOEs, hence, the resolution to improve their status was to privatize them. These institutions, especially the energy sector, are struggling to meet the demands of multiple policy goals and the business objectives needed to reconcile. According to Kikeri [26], SOEs often incurred substantial financial losses and became an unsustainable burden on the national budget and banking system. A case in point is the failure of electricity supply by Eskom, SABC mismanagement, SAA's instability to maintain air routes, SANRAL failure to collect revenue to sustain the E-Toll roads project, TRANSNET's failure to sustain the railroads, and others. There is a loss of revenue on the side of these entities due to these bad practices, and all these acts reduced business confidence and downgraded the South African economic outlook.

The Presidential Commission was tasked to investigate the performance of the SOEs in 2014. According to the Presidential Review Commission Report [27], the nonsupport and compliance of the government policies in support of SOEs slow down the successful application of CG in the SOEs. The overarching responsibilities of the board of directors and the financial disclosure were the main hiccup in the application of CG. The private sector, performed well as compared to public agencies and parastatals in the application of CG while there is limited potential for expansion of the private sector [27]. These predicaments faded the mandate of the energy sector to improve performance by exposing SOEs to competition, daunting budget allocations, and mismanagement of funds with staggering managerial changes. Padayachee [28] alluded to the absence of strong CG measures before 1994 and asserts that the arrival of the King IV Report on CG progressed toward a capable and valuable tool toward strong CG. The current involvement of the SOE's mismanagement of funds is revealed through the Public Protector Report [29] and Venter ([30], pp. 1–4) of the State Capture probe. These reports conveyed serious allegations of noncompliance to legal requirements like the PFMA and CG principles by the senior managers. A case in point is the continuous blackouts due to shortages of electricity supply by Eskom, and a weak administrative supply chain in government departments where these SOEs are managed.

2.3.2 Economic growth and transformation

The government's neoliberal policies impacted the SOE's performance, especially the New Growth Path (NGP), which was earmarked to create five million additional jobs by 2020. Other policies such as the National Development Plan (NDP), the Medium-Term Strategic Framework (MTSF), and the Industrial Policy Action Plan also focus on the role of SOEs as main suppliers to infrastructure development and economic restructuring, when the Nine-Point Plan, which focuses on the government priorities, includes tackling the electricity contest and backup of improvements in SOEs. Overall, the government's goal to guarantee the SOE's contributions toward the broader developmental goals and transformation was tested. The application of CG reveals weak systems of these SOEs, especially on the board performance on issues of financial disclosure and accountability to support the transformation and competitiveness of the economy.

Several SOEs in SA are managed through CG since they are commercialized and separate legal entities in the early 1980s after the integration of homeland parastatals into South African SOEs. In the efforts to advance a developmental state, performance contracts were developed to monitor SOEs' performance and hold managers accountable for results while some of the managers had limited experience and qualifications to manage [31]. The improvements in the SOEs fall short of expected targets in the current decade; hence, some of them from the energy and transport sector applied for financial bailouts. According to Kikeri [26], SOEs board of directors failed these entities, the early reforms were not all successful, and their implementation fell short while the senior managers were paid luxury salaries to fund their expensive life.

Even though the government bailed out some of the SOEs, some are still bankrupt, especially the energy sector. According to the IMF [32], the SOEs from the energy and transport sector are in the spotlight in South Africa due to their inconsistent performance in a staggering economy. Some of those SOEs from the utility sector include the electricity (Eskom) and water enterprises (i.e., the water boards and the Transcaledon Tunnel Authority (TCTA), a related water infrastructure company). The transport sector comprises mainly commercial railways, infrastructure on ports and pipelines (Transnet), airlines (SAA and SAX) and the related airport, air traffic and navigation companies (ACSA, ATNS), and passenger railway transportation (PRASA). Several Auditor's General's Reports (2019/2020) indicate mismanagement of funds and a decrease in investment ensuring the maintenance of some of these entities, while there are less or no benefits to the South African economy. According to Matsiliza [33], the mismanagement of funds by the SOEs led to financial bankruptcy in some of the SOEs. As a result, the government bailed out some entities, especially in the energy sector like Eskom.

2.3.3 Oversight and accountability

The SOEs are governed by some pieces of legislation created by the government such as the enabling legislation (EL), the Companies Act (CA), and the Public Finance Management Act (PFMA). Application of the EL differs across SOEs. EL can uphold the sort of SOE objectives and requirements on governance, oversight, reporting, and accountability. The CA determines the CG that can be applied to SOEs and private sector firms. The PFMA classifies the oversight responsibility for SOEs' shareholder compacts, corporate plans, and reporting requirements. The board members and the chief financial officers' responsibilities are classified in the PFMA. Also, the Cabinet adopted a protocol of CG which is a nonlegislated code of conduct to govern SOEs. There are diverse tools used to apply CG from various documents such as Kind 1–5 Reports, which define the relationship and balance between the government, SOEs, and stakeholders while pursuing the independence of SOEs from the executive in their day-to-day operations. According to the Zondo Commission Report on State Capture [11], there has been noncompliance and limited oversight of SOE for a long time.

The premier is a powerful representative and head of the province who has a legal right to monitor the financial viability of the SOEs/public entities at the provincial level and carries duties mandated by the Constitution [34]. The overseeing department at the provincial level will be responsible for the operation of the entity based on the directed services that are cut across various government departments. For instance, the South African National Road Agency (SANRAL) is a public agency that is responsible for the maintenance of road infrastructure in South Africa. It is monitored by the department of transport which has offices in all noni Provinces' route networks.

Legislative oversight through the parliament is complex in a bi-camera system that has two legislative chambers where the ruling party dominates in these chambers because it sets a motion that can always be accepted by the majority from the ruling party. The dominance of the ruling party on parliamentary oversight influences decision-making in parliament [35]. There is more influence on decision-making, especially on the functioning of parliamentary committees that are scheduled to investigate oversight and accountability matters of executive institutions and the SOEs. The separation of powers in South Africa should augment the role of the executive institutions in the monitoring of policy implementation in South Africa's public agencies. Even though the powers are separated between the legislative, executive, and judicial houses, they still work interdependently to enhance oversight and accountability. When there is a transgression of law by executives, the parliament can investigate the matter through parliamentary committees and submit recommendations to the president. Other institutions that assist in the oversight investigations in South Africa include the commissions appointed by the president, the National Prosecution Authority (NPA), and others. The oversight of Chapter 9 institutions and the SOEs are not a straight-train smash. Parties involved in the governance of these institutions have diverse interests in the governance of these enterprises. The provincial oversight is most centered around the premier house and the ministerial executing councils.

Parliament's Standing Committee on Public Accounts (SCOPA) is responsible for reviewing the SOE's annual financial statements and audit reports from the Auditor General. Each SOE sector accounts to separate portfolio committees that are charged to exercise oversight over corporate plans and targets of each SOEs service delivery performance. Each minister is responsible for ensuring policy alignment between SOEs and public departments to ensure proper corporate governance and to monitor policy implementation, respectively. The National Treasury and the Financial Ministry are answerable for financial oversight, especially on budget and spending to keep up with the national credit rating. The SOE boards of directors have full responsibility for the sustainability of these institutions by maintaining a balance between spending and performance to maintain a strategic direction for SOEs' performance. According to the IMF [32], SOEs in South Africa could have yielded better profits and outcomes if boards of directors, executive, and nonexecutive directors were skilled enough to manage risk and ensure that their key performance indicators are achieved timeously.

The involvement of politics deployed in the governance of SOE boards did not yield good results in investigating the corruption and mismanagement of SOEs. As reported by the Judicial Commission into the State Capture [11], the role of the ruling party is to safeguard the national interest in all its involvement in the parliamentary committees. It is alleged that some of the members presiding on these parliamentary committees overstepped their roles through a series of connections and relationships with the agency's stakeholders and service providers who ultimately influenced decision-making in the appointments of executive officials that manages the SOEs [31].

The involvement of agencies to make decisions on behalf of the state complicated exercise of autonomy in commercial decision-making. There is an existence of social responsibility adds value to the corporate governance of the SOEs but there was a thin line in the separation of commercial and social objectives. The State Capture Commission Report [11] also noted the requirements for the party's disclosure of assets and donations through their treasury General and their subcommittees on finance should be there to avoid the conflict of interest when the members have to account in parliament. This also settles the public service obligations by the members of the executive when transferring resources to the SOEs. While financial discipline and ethical leadership are required as ingredients in achieving good governance, greater autonomy for SOEs is reciprocal to having performance contracts, auditing, and good accountability mechanisms. A bad rating on the economic performance in South Africa could not support the transformation and reforms of SOEs. Continued economic degrading by other companies, like S&T and Moody, impacted negatively on the credit rating also of SOEs and the future economic outlook.

2.3.4 Leadership and governance of SOEs

The SOEs are governed mostly through Kings Reports (1–5), while there is no specific legislation that governs them and that imposed risk for the SOEs to efficiently achieve their goals through CG. Various acts regulate these enterprises such as the Companies Act, and the Public Financial Management Act. The rest of the inefficiencies and financial losses may result from conflicting interests that are wedged between all parties involved. Consequently, the principal–agent issue arises. Promoting privatization and agency theories is appropriate for this chapter to provide theoretical lenses and scholarly perspectives that could advance the debate on the pros and cons of corporate governance in South Africa's emerging economy and the broader society. Since private interests were already protected through foreign investment and the private sector, the establishment of a mixed economy in South Africa was not unexpected.

Ethical leadership seems to be a challenge, where there are business transactions with less or no accountability for the acts of the executives and senior managers in these entities. The contestations on privatization signaled fear from the society about the negative effects of privatization. The costs of privatization had long-term effects on the increased infrastructure and tariffs, losses of jobs due to restructuring and downsizing, and rising foreign ownerships since the selling of shares was open to global buyers. Kikeri and Nellis [36] and Nellis [37] argue that there was no proper planning for the privatization of SOEs. The process was neither favorable to the government nor to other shareholders, hence, the process ended up with scandals and mismanagement of resources when the institutional frameworks were lacking [38]. However, the whole process ended up questioning the role of the state.

2.4 Policy implications

It surfaced earlier that the understanding of CG is moderate; therefore, government officials and nonexecutive managers need continuous training and capacity building to allow change and development in the SOEs. The government must formulate legislation/policy that will directly regulate the SOEs without excluding the corporate governance principles that are already in place. Most SOEs are also regulated by diverse legal principles and policies such as the Public Financial Management (1994), Company Act (2008), and others. These policies enable oversight and accountability of executives in these entities. Other countries can also learn from the South African case, especially on how the gaps can be addressed. The policy implications are diverse, although it seems that CG is an effective tool for managing private companies, it is complex to manage state-owned enterprises with CG to improve investments in the other due to political interference.

The measuring and evaluation of the performance of SOEs in South Africa need to be examined. As it has also been daunted by the political forces since most of the committee members and board members have political allegiance to the ruling party, they find it difficult to report early financial entanglements and misuse of public resources that hurt the country's investment [39]. Investigating on the integrity of institutions and the Judicial Commissions, they should ask themselves questions on whether they need to adopt Corporate Government in these entities the same way as they are applied in private companies. Another important policy implication is on finding qualified and skilled managers that will also understand policy directives and be able to assist the government in formulating tools that will be directed at measuring performance and monitoring the SOEs. The Zondo Judicial Commission [40] found discrepancies in the management of SOEs, where the executives were involved in service delivery contracts for personal gains [40].

3. Conclusion

CG has been adopted to steer the SOEs on the right path from the early days of democracy in South Africa. This chapter demonstrated that parastatals/SOEs experienced unstable growth and development due to the impact of socioeconomic and political influence in government decisions to sustain these entities.

Among these factors, political oppositions contested the privatization of SOEs, especially in the energy and infrastructure sectors. SOEs have been exposed to loss of scrutiny since the government is the majority controlling shareholder.

Corruption and maladministration in SOEs demonstrate self-sabotage of the South African democracy. The allegations on Zondo Judicial Commission imply a weak supply chain system, and the absence of a direct legislation or policy to direct/guide and monitor the performance of SOE instead of relying on corporate governance only.

The global financial crisis and the COVID-19 epidemic affected the operation of public sector entities and added to their problems with the nondelivery of services to clients. The current challenge of SOEs emerged from their act of noncompliance of the shareholders and their executives to corporate governance principles. This chapter demonstrated the challenges of CG in the South African SOEs with special reference to accountability and oversight mechanisms.

3.1 Recommendations

Even though SOEs are not perfect in the application compliance and accountability mechanisms, these elements pressured governments all over the world to turn their attention back to enhancing SOE performance. Despite widespread privatization, SOEs' Function and Value Governments still own and run national commercial companies in crucial industries including finance, infrastructure, manufacturing, energy, and natural resources. State-owned industries have persisted and even grown in many low- and middle-income nations, significant emerging market economies, and high-income nations. A considerable number of SOEs are currently among the biggest investors, businesses, and participants in the capital markets worldwide. SOEs in vital industries are increasingly seen as instruments for faster development and international expansion in many nations. South African government must learn lessons from the progressive global SOEs and improve their performance.

Lessons can also be learned from other African and global SOEs on the employment of competent and specialized managers in risk, accounting, and other operations. The government in its new path of renewal must provide continuous training to the managers, executives, and nonexecutives charged to manage the SOEs.

They must match and place employees well in the suitable positions. It is also imperative for government to introduce a merit-based cadre deployment of encumberments to improve their skills and performance.

Integrity institutions and the justice system need to upscale their capacity and pace of correcting the wrongdoings as findings of the investigation on the alleged corruption and mismanagement of funds in the SOEs, by strengthening the prosecution and instilling ethical culture and compliance measurements in the SOEs.

External forces such as political interference impact the business of SOEs and can only be minimized when risk assessment is prioritized. The SOEs must hire qualified and skilled risk managers to assess and manage risk and compliance at all phases of major projects such as infrastructure, roads, and energy. Evidence on the mistakes of limited oversight and risk management can provide lessons from the energy side by Eskom risk managers who failed to estimate future shortages of energy and power supply of electricity in South Africa.

Author details

Noluthando Shirley Matsiliza
University of Fort Hare, Alice, Eastern Cape Province, South Africa

*Address all correspondence to: thandimatsi@yahoo.co; thandimatsi@yahoo.co.za

References

[1] Li MH, Cui L, Lu J. Varieties in state capitalism: Outward FDI strategies of central and local state-owned enterprises from emerging economy countries. In: State- Owned Multinationals. Cham: Palgrave Macmillan; 2018. pp. 175-210

[2] Cuervo-Cazurra A, Inkpen A, Musacchio A, Ramaswamy K. Governments as owners: State-owned multinational companies. Journal of International Business Studies. 2014;**45**:919-942

[3] Mtshali MS. A policy analysis of state-owned enterprises: The case study of South African national road agency limited (SANRAL) [Unpublished doctoral thesis]. South Africa: University of KwaZulu-Natal; 2016

[4] Bryman A, Bell B, Hirschsohn P, Santos D, Toit D. Research Methodology: Business and Management Contexts. Cape Town: Oxford University Press Southern Africa (Pty) Limited; 2014

[5] Organization for Economic Co-operation and Development. Stated-Owned Enterprises in the Development Process. 2015. pp. 1-59. OECD Website on Corporate Governance at http://www.oecd.org/corporate

[6] Bowen GA. Document analysis as a qualitative research method. Qualitative Research Journal. 2009;**9**(2):27-40

[7] Taylor S. Critical policy analysis: Exploring contexts, texts and consequences. Discourse: Studies in the Cultural Politics of Education. 1997;**18**(1):23-35

[8] Robinson S, Sun W, Arrigoni A. Editorial: Commentary on king reports on corporate governance. Journal of Global Responsibility. 2020;**11**(2):113-121. ISSN 2041-2568. DOI: 10.1108/jgr-05-2020-109

[9] Van Zyl M, Mans-Kemp N. Reflecting on corporate governance in South Africa: Lessons learned and the way forward. 2020

[10] Hollibaugh GE Jr, Rothenberg LS. The who, when, and where of executive nominations: Integrating Agency Independence and Appointee Ideology. American Journal of Political Science. 2018;**62**(2):296-311

[11] Republic of South Africa. The Judicial Commission Report on the State Capture. Pretoria: The Zondo Commission; 2022

[12] Sultan Balbuena S. State-owned Enterprises in Southern Africa: A stocktaking of reforms and challenges. In: OECD Corporate Governance Working Papers, No. 13. Paris: OECD Publishing; 2014. DOI: 10.1787/5jzb5zntk5r8-en

[13] Sarika PR, James NR. Polyelectrolyte complex nanoparticles from cationised gelatin and sodium alginate for curcumin delivery. Carbohydrate Polymers. 2016;**148**:354-361

[14] Weber L, Duderstadt JJ, editors. Global Sustainability and the Responsibilities of Universities. London, UK: Economical; 2012

[15] Atinyo D, Kawor S. Relationship between corporate governance and financial crisis: A study of Ghana's banking sector. The International Journal of Business & Management. 2022;**10**(2)

[16] Ong T, Djajadikerta HG. An empirical analysis of corporate

governance and sustainability reporting in the Australian resources industry. Social Responsibility Journal. 2018

[17] Tariq YB, Ejaz A, Bashir MF. Convergence and compliance of corporate governance codes: A study of 11 Asian emerging economies. Corporate Governance: The International Journal of Business in Society. 2022 (ahead-of-print)

[18] Amartey LA, Yu M, Chukwu-lobelu O. Corporate governance in Ghana: An analysis of board accountability in Ghanaian listed banks. Journal of Financial Regulation and Compliance. 2019;**27**(2):126-140

[19] Agyei-Mensah BK. The relationship between corporate governance, corruption and forward-looking information disclosure: A comparative study. Corporate Governance: The International Journal of Business in Society. 2017

[20] Gurumoorthi. Role: Oversight, Corporate Governance in Botswana. 2021. https://www.rsm.global/botswana/news/king-3-governance-code. [Assessed: December 9, 2021]

[21] Directors Institute of Botswana. Corporate governance in Botswana. 2021

[22] Magang TI, Magang VG. Corporate governance and compliance in Botswana: Issues and challenges. Journal of Research in Business, Economics and Management. 2016;7(1):1041-1061

[23] Muswere J, Dube ZL. An assessment of corporate governance practices of SOEs in Zimbabwe's ICT sector. African Journal of Development Studies (formerly AFFRIKA Journal of Politics, Economics and Society). 2022;**12**(3):167-187

[24] Josiah J, Themba D, Matenge TM. Corporate governance in Botswana: Exploring developments and compliance. Botswana Journal of Business. 2016;**9**(1):1-20

[25] Thabane T, van Deventer ES. Pathological corporate governance deficiencies in South Africa's state-owned companies: A critical reflection. Potchefstroom Electronic Law Journal/Potchefstroom's Elektroniese Regsblad. 2018;**21**(1)

[26] Kikeri S. Corporate Governance in South African State-Owned Enterprises. 2018

[27] The Republic of South Africa. Presidential Review Commission Report on the Categorisation of State-Owned Entities. Pretoria: Government Printers; 2015

[28] Padayachee V. King IV is here: Corporate governance in SA revisited. New Agenda: South African Journal of Social and Economic Policy. 2017;**2017**(66):17-21

[29] Public Protector. State of capture: Report on an investigation into alleged improper and unethical conduct by the President and other state functionaries relating to alleged improper relationships and involvement of the Gupta family in the removal and appointment of Ministers and Directors of State-Owned Enterprises resulting in the improper and possibly corrupt award of state contracts and benefits to the Gupta family's businesses. Report No 6 of 2016/17. 2016. p. 15

[30] Venter T. The Zondo Commission and the failure of political oversight. Farmer's Weekly. 2022;**2022**(22028):14

[31] February J. State capture: An entirely new type of corruption. ISS Southern Africa Report. 2019;**2019**(25):1-16

[32] International Monetary Fund. "State-Owned Enterprises: The Other

Government", Chapter 3. Fiscal Monitor, Fiscal Affairs Department; 2020

[33] Matsiliza NS. Corporate governance of the state-owned enterprises in an emerging country: Risk management and related issues. Risk Governance and Control: Financial Markets and Institutions. 2017;7(3):35-43

[34] The Republic of South Africa. The South African Constitution. Pretoria: Government Printers; 1996

[35] Madue SM. Complexities of the oversight role of legislatures. Journal of Public Administration (0036-0767). 2012;**47**(2):431

[36] Kikeri S, Nellis J. An assessment of privatization. The World Bank Research Observer. 2004;**19**(1):87-118

[37] Nellis J. Whatever Happened to Privatization? The World Bank and Divestiture. 2021

[38] Birdsall N, Nellis J. Privatization reality check: Distributional effects in developing countries. Preface. 2005;**vii**:1

[39] Madumi P. Are state-owned enterprises (SOEs) catalysts for or inhibitors of South African economic growth? International Conference on Public Administration and Development Alternatives (IPADA). 2018

[40] The Presidency. Judicial Commission Inquiry into the State Capture Report. Pretoria: The Presidency; 2022

Chapter 5

Perceptions of and Reactions to the HR Implementation Process in Nigeria

Paul Nwanna

Abstract

Leveraging attribution theories, this chapter examines the role of employees' cognitions in the HR implementation process in Nigeria. This study relies on secondary sources such as journal articles, textbooks and public service reforms to review the current state of HR practice. This review shows that while there is a continuous evolvement of HRM practices in Nigeria, its effectiveness to contribute to the strategic value of both public and private sector organisations is countered by socio-cognitive factors. Moreover, the analysis reveals different patterns of causal attributions in how workers interpret the goals of HR practices due to socio-cultural and economic factors that are unique to the Nigerian context. This chapter contributes to the international debates about the integration of contextual factors and HR processes in the conceptualisation of HRM effectiveness. The limitations of this review are discussed as well as the implications for future HR research.

Keywords: Nigeria, HR implementation, attribution theories, paternalism, ethnicity

1. Introduction

The free movement of capital across nations bears within itself the cross-border transfer of management systems, especially from more developed economies (e.g. UK and USA) to developing economies like Nigeria [1, 2]. This could be to replicate the tangible results witnessed by using the management systems of the West in another geographical context. However, there are questions about the transferability of HRM practices formulated in the western context to disparate national context [3–5]. Typically, HRM research in developing countries like Nigeria has pointed to the intersection of local customs and values, institutions, economic conditions, and legislations in the evaluation of HRM in Africa [6–8]. Although examining these macro contextual factors (e.g. national cultures and regulative institutions, etc.) is useful in understanding the effects of HRM, it does not fully explain 'how' such effect is achieved. In particular, research has yet to investigate the (micro) socio-cognitive processes involved in how employees interpret HR practices in an African context. As such, the first objective of this chapter is to explicate the role of the employee attribution process in the evaluation of Anglo-American-developed HRM in the African context. This is likely to account for the salient cognitive complexities associated with how an employee formulate a belief about their organisation's intent to select specific HR practices. Examining employee cognitions of HR practices in Nigeria is theoretically important, as they are critical in theorising the effect of HRM on organisational outcomes [9]. In addition, there are recent calls in the renowned Academy of Management Journal Proceedings (e.g. [10]) and Human resources Journals (e.g. [9]) to examine the role of HR attribution in the link between HRM and organisational performance to provide a nuanced understanding of the HR processes in organisation. As such, this chapter utilises attribution theories [11–13] to analyse the effects of contextual factors on the employees' causal attribution of HR practices in Nigeria.

In addition, although initial research on HRM in the Nigerian context (e.g. [14, 15]) have reported a positive relationship between HR practices and organisation performance, little is known about the role of the line manager in the relationship in Nigerian context. Research on HRM devolution has suggested that line managers are the bridge between HRM strategy, policies, and practices and the bottom-line employees' performance. Bos-Nehles et al. [16] defined a line manager as the (bottom-line) manager who manages a team of operational employees daily and is responsible for performing HRM activities (p. 256). Line managers, in comparison to HR managers/professionals, are considered better positioned in an organisation to understand employees' competencies and concerns, and to implement HR strategy, policies, and practice more effectively for better motivational and behavioural outcomes [17]. Indeed, research reports have shown that line managers' HR implementation influences employee perception of HRM practice and, in turn, leads to motivation, satisfaction, and performance [17]. As such, the second objective of this chapter is to highlight the role of line managers in organisation's context with specific consideration of socio-cultural factors that influence the line manager's leadership behaviour in the HR implementation process.

Based on the above objectives, this chapter has two main contributions. First, it presents a theoretical framework that has the potential to explain how the regulative and social-cultural institutions influence on employees' perceptions and reactions to HR practices in Nigeria's context. Secondly, it contributes to HRM research by acknowledging the role of line managers as well as the value of employee attributions to the understanding of the HR process and outcomes in a different national context.

Nigeria is the most populous black Nation in the world, with an estimated population of 211 million people, of which 85.41% are of working age [18]. She gained her independence from British colonial rule in 1960 but plunged into civil war from 1967 to 1970. She has since interspersed between democratically elected civilian governments to military dictatorships until she gained a stable constitutional democracy in 1999. The country has the largest GDP in West Africa [18] and its economy is largely dependent on crude oil export, accounting for about 85 percent of government revenues. She has other natural resources like gold, cocoa, limestone, lead, coal and iron ore, etc. [19]. Over the years, Nigeria has instituted several neo-liberal economic policies and practices to diversify the economy and to create market-oriented systems through privatisation, deregulation, and liberalisation [20]. With its vast natural and human resources base as well as numerous economic reforms, Nigeria has become one of the most attractive destinations for foreign investors in Africa, especially in the sector of energy, banking, telecommunications, etc. Accordingly, Nigeria is the third host economy for foreign direct investments (FDI) in Africa after Egypt and Ethiopia [21]. Despite the negative effects of the Coronavirus pandemic on the global economy, the total flow of FDI to Nigeria in 2020 was USD 2.4 Billion, which was a 3.5% increment compared to the previous year, which stood at USD 2.3 billion [21]. Some of the main investing countries in Nigeria are the USA, China, the United Kingdom, the Netherlands, and France. The influx of these foreign investors into the local market has put indigenous companies under pressure to imitate the "best HR practices" to survive the strong competition posed by multinational companies [22]. For example, Anakwe [23] adopting convergence, divergence and cross-vergence perspectives [24, 25] reported that Nigeria has a cross-vergence HRM system, which is a blend of human resource management of both generalised western HR practices and localised practices. As such, Nigeria is an interesting national context to extrapolate the investigation of employee HR attribution because the country has both developed and rudimentary HR practices, which could offer new insights into how employees formulate their perceptions, interpretations, and beliefs about their organisation's HR practices.

As HRM research in the Nigerian context often focused on the analysis of macro contextual factors, this chapter reviews the two main contextual factors. First, HRM research in Nigeria has examined the effectiveness of formal institutions (e.g. labour unions, economy, and legislation) to enhance human resource development and fair employee relations (e.g. [26]). For example, research has reported that legislative acts, such as Labour Act 2004 and the Workers Compensation Act, 2010, are poorly enforced because of endemic corruption that bedevilled the government institutions [22, 27]. Further, mass unemployment, which currently stands at 33.3% [28], has also hindered workers from demanding their basic rights from employing organisations [22]. Similarly, studies have reported that the trade unions that were established, along industry lines, to ensure that workers express their concerns and grievances are losing their bargaining power due to high levels of unemployment and corruption among trade union leaders [29]. Indeed, these contextual factors have created a work environment where stakeholders' values are prioritised over employee needs. On another note, research has found that informal contextual factors such as culture, religion, ethnicity, and linguistic affinity influence employees' perceptions and reactions to HRM in Nigeria [26]. There are three major ethnic groups in Nigeria namely Hausa-Fulani, Yoruba, Igbo, and over 200 minority ethnic groups. These ethnic groupings differ in culture, religion, and sometimes even in physical features [30]. In particular, research reports have suggested that ethnic, religious, and social diversity play significant roles in the rise of nepotism, corruption, tribalism, favouritism, and political intrusion affecting the quality of HR implementation in Nigeria [22, 26].

Given the contextual factors affecting HR practice in Nigeria, this chapter will organise the rest of the review into six sections. First, I will provide a clear overview of both formal and informal factors associated with five traditional HR practices in Nigeria. Second, I will discuss the role of the line manager in HR implementation in Nigeria. This will reveal the devolved HR practices in Nigeria's organisations and shape our understanding of the implications of contextual factors in the HR implementation process. Third, I will present an overview of attribution theories to enable us to understand the basic assumptions of different attribution theories and their past applications in HRM research. In the fourth section, I will evaluate how attributions theories can be applied to explain employees' perceptions and reactions to implemented HR practices in.

Nigeria. The fifth section will state the implications of this review for future HRM research while the sixth section will discuss its limitations. Finally, I conclude by reiterating how the employee HR attribution process shapes HRM practices.

2. HRM in Nigeria: an overview

HRM is rooted in the idea that 'people' are a valuable asset that when managed effectively can contribute to the strategic goals of an organisation. Indeed, it is argued that organisations can leverage people-focused management practices to achieve competitive advantage over their counterparts, especially when other sources of competitive advantage (e.g. technology) can be easily replicated [31]. However, there is a lack of consensus on what constitutes the human resource practices among management scholars. For this review, I will focus on the five traditional HR practices and evaluate the contextual factors that affect the application of each of them in Nigeria.

2.1 Recruitment and selection

In a study that examined HRM practices in Nigeria and Ghana, Arthur et al. [32] reported that newspaper advertisements dominated recruitment strategy for most organisations, followed by written notices in and around the organisations, employment agencies, announcements in professional/trade publications and visits to university and college campuses. HR managers also receive unsolicited applications because of the high employment rate in the country.

In terms of selection, the centralised HR department is responsible for designing and administering this process while a smaller percentage of the organisation relies on external agencies [32]. The selection interview is given much preference, followed by academic qualification, and a letter of recommendation. The decision to hire employees is normally made by the HR manager while the decision to hire a managerial-level employee is made by top management with the consultation of the HR manager [33].

However, due to poor institutional regulations, organisations sometimes rely on informal HRM practices such as recruitment based on social networks, and ethnic and personal affiliations [26]. This is prevalent in public sector organisations where the state of origin, hometown, and ethnic group of job applicants are considered of equal relevance with competency, qualification, and talent [27]. Even the entrenchment of the quota system of employment based on principles of inclusion (i.e. an expression of federal character) to resolve this skewed employment system has been poorly implemented. Hence, this has caused disharmony and infighting among workers and poor performance standards [27].

2.2 Performance appraisal

There is wide use of the formal system in evaluating employee performance in Nigeria. According to Arthur, et al. [32], most organisations in Nigeria use performance appraisal information for personnel decisions such as for promotion and transfer. Some organisations use it for employee feedback while few organisations use it for personnel research. Supervisors' ratings of employee performance and personnel-based data (absenteeism and commendation) are largely used by organisations while some use objective performance data such as sales data [32]. Only a few organisations use self-rating, customer rating, subordinate rating, and peer rating. However, Nigeria is a high power distance [34], a cultural orientation that emphasises a top-down relationship between an employer and employees, and a collectivist culture, a cultural orientation that emphasises the value of utilising work groups to complete tasks and an expression of a communitarian spirit both in the workplace and in communities. Based on these cultural orientations, most performance appraisal processes in Nigeria assumed a top-down pattern and team-based systems [35]. Moreover, the traditional values of communitarianism make it difficult for line managers to give negative feedback or conduct a face-to-face appraisal as it may be considered an attempt to ruin someone's career [36]. As such, some organisations like commercial banks use ranking methods, with a specific focus on employee financial performance in an attempt to maintain objectivity [35].

2.3 Training and development

Most organisations in Nigeria conduct training for their employees. In their study, Arthur et al. [32] reported that there is a formally stated policy on training, a separate training department, a separate training budget, and training facilities and use of external training specialists or consultants in most Nigerian organisations. On-the-job training is mostly used by organisations while lectures and discussions, and job rotations are minimally used [32]. Large organisations such as financial institutions are likely to combine these training methods to ensure an appropriate harnessing of human capital. For example, First Bank Nigeria established training schools across the country (e.g. Lagos, Ibadan, Kano, and Benin City). They structured their Training and Development Programme along with employee job-specific skills, knowledge-based training, and self-development [37]. After the induction of a new employee in which he/she learns about the policies, procedures, and practices of the Bank, he/she undergoes on-the-job training then he/she will go for external training at one of these training centres across Nigeria. At the training centre, the new employee goes through a series of training based on their job description such that a customer-contact employee will attend a Clerical Operations Course, Cashier Training Course, and IT and Customer Service Training Course. The bank also encourages the employee to take self-development programs with provision for reimbursement on tuition and examination fees. There is a prospect of promotion and increment of appropriate salary scale following these pieces of training.

In the public sector, government-training institutes such as the Public Service Institute of Nigeria, the National Institute for Public Information, the Foreign Service Academy, and the Institute for Labour Studies was established to provide capacity building for public service employees. There are also opportunities for senior managers to attend overseas training institutes funded by the government. In addition, the increase in global interest in human capital building in developing economies prompted international development agencies like United Nations Development programs, International Labour Organisation, and the World Bank to fund training programmes for public sector employees. However, Nigeria still suffers shortages in skill and human capital development. According to UNDP's Human Development Index in 2021 [38], Nigeria with a 0.535 HDI value ranks 163 out of 191 against other countries. Scholars have traced this unfortunate situation to the adoption of neo-liberal policies, which exerted pressure on the government to cut down on their spending on critical areas of the economy such as education and health [26]. To compensate for this low human capital development, private organisations tend to invest huge resources in the training and development of their employees [22].

2.4 Pay and rewards

Performance or merit-based systems dominate the reward system in Nigeria [32]. However, there are variations in the pay and rewards system in the public and private sector organisations in Nigeria. The public sector operates a service-wide remuneration so that variations (including across gender) based on performance are non-existent. Rather, the national minimum wage (with fringe benefits) and legally mandated leaves such as paid maternity and annual leave are the basis of the payment and reward system. The minimum wage is the basis for negotiations between trade unions and employers. In the private sector, the pay and reward system is mostly determined by employees' level of experience, educational qualifications, and skill sets. Workers also get some fringe benefits such as the allocation of company vehicles for senior staff, car loans, paid leave, and paid gym membership.

Nigeria's cultural values play a considerable role in the payment and rewards systems. Based on the principles of communitarianism, there is a tendency for workers to view organisations as an extension of their extended family, where their material and socio-emotional needs as well as family and personal circumstances are considered when making personnel decisions [36]. In keeping with this focus, some organisations have introduced burial allowances and compassionate leave for employees who are bereaved of their loved ones to help them cope with the expenses of elaborate burial ceremonies. Similar gestures are shown to workers who are getting married to help with their wedding expenses [36]. In most cases, the organisation also appoints fellow employees to attend these ceremonies in a show of solidarity and support for the concerned employees.

2.5 Employee involvement

In Nigeria, the management systems adopted by the public and private sectors differ in the degree of employee involvement in the work process. Public sector organisations follow a unitary system and a bureaucratic model of employment whereby the organisation's employment decisions are centralised and the administrative system follows strict bureaucratization of procedures. As such, employees' inputs are not considered in the decision-making and work processes. Rather, the organisation's policies dictate the employees' behaviour, with line managers expected to implement and enforce the rule-governed policies. Although line managers could hold meetings to discuss emergent issues with the employees, they are mostly to provide clear directions about employee performance expectations and goals.

In the private sector context, employee involvement varies based on organisational type, size, and employee position in the organisation. While consulting firms and other medium-size organisations may consider their employees' input in the decision-making process, large organisations rarely require their employees opinions in making decisions about the work process. In most cases, employees at the lowest level are expected to follow the directions of their line manager in executing their tasks while team leaders' opinions may be considered. However, as Nigeria is a high power distance culture [34], there is a tendency for managers to resist employee involvement in the decision-making process as this may reduce their power of influence in the organisation [15].

The next section evaluates the role of line managers in the HR implementation process. Line managers are closest to employee experience in the HR implementation process. As such, presenting an overview of the role of line managers in HR implementation in Nigeria will clear the path for a good understating of the HR implementation process in the country.

3. Line manager role in HRM implementation in Nigeria

As HRM continued to evolve in the Nigerian context, HR practices are increasingly devolved to the line managers across different types of organisations. In small enterprises, the owner-manager is responsible for HR implementation. This informal HR system the approach is most evident in the Igbo (a tribe in Nigeria) apprenticeship the system, "a communal enterprising framework where successful businesses develop others and overtime provides capital and gives away their customers to the new business" ([39] p. 1). Typically, a business owner recruits an apprentice, mainly through family and social connections, and provides vocational training through peer mentoring, rewarding the apprentice based on traditional values of communitarianism. This system is considered to ensure the stability and longevity of family business networks and performance. On the other hands, large corporations such as energy, banking, and the telecommunication sector, etc., have a formal approach to HR implementation, with HR departments and line managers playing key roles in HR enactment. For example, Jimoh, and Danlami [40] reported that, in Nigeria's manufacturing sectors, HR practices such as employee training, recruitment, and selection of new employees, performance appraisal, and design job roles are increasingly devolved to the line managers (with the coordination of the HR department) because they consider HR devolution as part of their HR strategy. In the banking sector, however, line managers' role in the HR implementation is limited to on-the-job training, employee relation, performance appraisal, and individualised pay awards while the HR department is responsible for administrative functions such as recruitment, payroll, and external training [41]. HR departments also provide clear direction and adequate training the line managers to execute their 'newly' devolved HR practices, as a lack of HR-related competencies and skills is likely the affect their effectiveness in the HR implementation process [42].

However, the high level of unemployment in Nigeria and the pressure to meet competing business (e.g. quality and productivity) demands alongside HR activities may affect the way line managers implement HR practices [42] For example, line managers may enact HR practices with a focus on short-term goals over the long-term strategic vision of their organisation. They also may behave inconsistently and thus, deviates from the strategic goals of their organisation. Under this circumstance, scholars have suggested HR department HR specialists/HR departments and line managers should form a partnership in developing and managing HR practices to achieve a unitarist approach to people management [42].

The next session draws from attribution theory to evaluate employees' perceptions and reactions to the context and line manager in the HR implementation process in Nigeria. Before that, it is important to present an overview of attribution theories in HRM literature. This will help organise our thoughts about key factors that are involved in attribution processes.

4. The overview of attribution theory

The basic premise of attribution theory is that people have an innate desire to control the events around them and to understand the causality of their behaviour and that their attribution influences their responses to them and future behaviour [43]. Attribution theory has been applied, inter alia, to understand the HRM process [9] and the leadership process [44]. There are three foremost contributors to the theoretical development of attribution theory. First, Heider [11] argued that people's attributions are dependent on whether the locus of causality for their behaviour is dependent on the person, the environment, or both. The internal locus of causality consists of both motivations and ability while the external locus of causality includes situational factors such as opportunity etc. For example, when an employee misses his/her performance targets, the manager will use the information about his/her motivation, ability, and situational factors (lack of requisite physical resources) to infer the causality of the employee performance failure. In addition, Heider [11] extended the attribution theory by examining errors that may occur during the attribution process. The first is the *fundamental attribution error*, which occurs when individuals ascribe the causality of an individual's behaviour to internal factors, rather than external factors. The second attribution error is the *actor-observer effect*. This error describes the inclination for an actor to ascribe the causality of their behaviour to external factors while an observer makes causal inferences of the same behaviour to internal factors [45]. Lastly, self-serving bias is the tendency for an actor to attribute the causality of their behaviour for positive events to internal factors while negative events are ascribed to external factors [46]. This attribution perspective has been applied to explain interpersonal dynamics and attribution of behaviour/event within several specific HR functions, such as performance management, grievances, disciplinary actions, recruitment and selection, training, and occupational health and safety (see [10]).

Kelley [12] expanded on Heider's attribution theory by evaluating the information pattern that people use to make causal attribution, known as the covariation principle (e.g. consensus, consistency, and distinctiveness information). Distinctiveness refers to the extent to which a person behaves in a similar way across identical situations. Consensus refers to the extent to which there is a collective agreement in the observation of different people about a person's behaviour. Consistency refers to the extent to which an individual behaves in the same way over time. Kelley [12] noted that when people have access to multiple cases of similar behaviour and events, they would use a different combination of information patterns to infer whether the individual behaviour is caused by internal (disposition) and external (situation) factors [43]. An observer is likely to infer the causes of a person's behaviour to internal factors when there is low distinctiveness, high consistency, and high consensus [47]. Bowen and Ostroff [48] adopted this Kelley's [12] covariation principle (and Michel's [49] situational strength) perspective to conceptualise how consistent, distinctive, and consensus HRM messages affect the strength of the relationship between HRM and organisational performance, conceptually framed as *HR system strength*.

Finally, Weiner [13] extended Heider and Kelley's works by examining the consequences of causal attributions as well as how dimensions (e.g. locus of causality, stability, and controllability) of attributional explanation (e.g. effort, ability, luck, and task difficulty) could affect emotion and behaviour. He argued that different combinations of locus of causality, stability, and controllability in an achievement context is associated with attributions of ability, effort, task the difficulty, and luck [13]. Nishii et al. [50] partly adopted Weiner's [13] attributional theory explains how employees' subjective interpretation of HR practices influences their attitudinal and behavioural reactions towards it. Nishii et al. [50] noted that employees could make either internal or external attributions about the purpose of HR policies and practices, which could result in the attachment of different meanings and behaviours.

Accordingly, when employees make positive internal HR attribution that their management's intent for designing HR practices is to enhance service quality and well-being, they are likely to develop positive perceptions, attitudes, and behaviour towards their management's goals. Conversely, when employees make negative internal HR attribution that their management's intent for designing HR practices are to reduce cost and for exploitation, they will develop negative perceptions, attitudes, and behaviour towards their management goals. Similarly, when an individual makes an external HR attribution that the management intents for designing HR practices to comply with union requirements, they will also develop a negative perception, attitude, and behaviour towards the management goals [50].

5. Analyses of employee perceptions and reactions in the HR implementation process in Nigeria

As already stated, Heider, Kelly, and Weiner's attribution theories provide a theoretically an informed understanding of the cognitive complexities associated with the HR implementation process in Nigeria. One notable HR practice that can be explained using these attribution theories are the recruitment and selection strategy. The purpose of recruitment in organisations is to inject new ideas and creativity into the work and productive process of organisations. In Nigeria's context, the ethnic, economic, religious, and tribal bias may have implications on how employees make causal attribution about the goals of their organisation's recruitment and selection practices. Specifically, there is a the tendency for an applicant to ascribe the causality of his/her success in a job application to an external factor (e.g. social affiliations), and may perceive it as a form of social obligation on the part of the employer, who in the communitarian spirit is responsible to care for his/her family and acquaintances. This cognitive formulation may instil a high level of affective trust between the employer and the applicant but may negatively affect the quality of the human resource base of the organisation. On the other hand, an applicant that ascribes the causality for his/her successful job application to internal factors (ability e.g. qualifications) may view the recruitment strategy as an effective organisational practice and feel appreciated for having the relevant skills for the job. This causal analysis is more informative due to the stability and controllability (internal factors) of the cause for the successful job application. In another scenario, an applicant, though possessing the relevant skill for the job may ascribe their success to external factors (luck or divine intervention) because of the high level of unemployment, poor institutional regulations, and the highly competitive labour market in Nigeria. These type of applicants normally express their joy by giving testimonies/thanksgiving in religious centres to celebrate their newfound jobs. In this context, applicants can make *a fundamental attribution error,* which is, ascribing the causality of their success to external factors (luck), rather than internal factors (qualification). There is also the possibility of error of *the actor-observer effect* to occur because the applicant ascribed his/her success to an external factor (luck) while the employer hired him/her based on an internal factor (qualification). *Self-serving bias* may also occur because the applicant may attribute their success to an internal factor (qualification) while their lack of success may be attributed to external factors (e.g. lack of social affiliations to the employer).

These variations in the applicants' causal attribution is likely to be exacerbated based on the information pattern they applied in the attribution process. In keeping with Kelly's [12] covariation principle, an applicant that observes the recruitment and selection strategy to be distinctively low (low distinctiveness), that is, the organisation hires people based on their ethnic and social affiliation with the employer (or other top executives) across different times; high consensus – applicants, during socialisation, collectively agree on the skewness of the recruitment and selection strategy towards ethnicity; high consistency – the organisation always hires people from the employer's ethnic group, they are likely to ascribe the cause of their success to external factors. This causal analysis is likely to cause disaffection among employees, cause poor performance standards, and high turnover intention. In practical terms, this attribution process is likely to be more evident in Nigerian civil service as people from the family and ethnicity of the incumbent heads tends to dominate departments [51]. It is noted, "In some places, 'the ethnic tongue' of the boss (i.e. his local language) is the *de facto lingua franca* in the office" ([52], p. 184). Personnel of the same ethnic stock as the boss are prioritised to occupy strategic positions in the department even before his/her seniors. They are also selected over their peers to attend overseas training and are recommended for special recognition without following standard procedure and practice. Thus, Olugbile [53] observed that 'nepotism had shaded into ethnicity in Nigeria' (p. 13) and this has resulted in maladministration, absenteeism, tardiness, inefficiency, and discontent among workers in the Nigerian public sector.

A similar trend exists in the private sector but not on the same magnitude. Private organisations exist to maximise profit unlike the public sector - which is focused on efficiency, value, and quality [54]. As such, they are under pressure to recruit, select and develop their human resource capability to meet their market and economic goals. As such, prioritising ethnic and familial affiliations over qualifications (and capacity) in their recruitment and selection strategy may adversely affect the quality of their human resources base, and eventually their business outcomes. Given this hindsight, the information pattern applied in the attribution process in the private sector employees may be different compared to the public sector. There might be low distinctiveness – organisation hires people based on their ethnic and social affiliation with the employer (or other top executives) across different times; low consensus – applicants, during socialisation, do not collectively agree that the organisation hires them based on their ethnicity; low consistency – the organisation does not always hire people from the employer's ethnic group. In this context, they may ascribe the cause of their success in the job application to internal factors (qualification/capability). This cognitive expression is likely to cultivate the belief in employees that the organisation prioritises their human resource capacity over ethnic/social factors, which in turn, translates to better motivational and performance outcomes. Another contextual stimulus that may shape an employee's causal attribution is the line manager's leadership behaviour at the operational level [17]. Leadership behaviours are considered responsible for the discretionary application of specific HR practices to individual employees [17]. For example, the line manager's leadership behaviour considers the employee's job experience and skill level in the allocation of a task. Leadership behaviours also signify an interpretive filter that aligns HRM messages to employee actual employee experience, attitude, and behaviour [48, 55]. However, cross-cultural research in leadership has suggested that cultural differences could hinder an individual's perception of leadership effectiveness in Nigeria [56]. The concept of leadership in the West African context, like Nigeria, is deeply embedded in the collectivist orientation that is manifested in familial, paternalistic, and communitarian dispositions [57]. An expression of this culturally endorsed leadership style is likely to spill over to how employees perceive the effectiveness of HR practices, and their motivation and performance. Therefore, a line manager's leadership behaviour that emphasises paternalistic orientation with a focus on the humanistic view of human value is likely to signal to employees more culturally fit HR practices, design for their development, and career success as well as meeting performance-driven goals. Paternalism refers to a simultaneous display of authoritarian and benevolent styles of leadership; it is characterised by centralised decision-making, with subordinates expected to implement those decisions if they are to be favoured by the leader [58]. However, as Nigeria is a socially dependent society, line managers' selective display of authoritarian and benevolent leadership in the enactment of HR practices across individuals in a team is likely to send mixed signals about the goal of HR practices [59].

Following Nishii et al. [50] HR attribution, a line manager that displays differentiated autocratic/benevolent leadership behaviour towards an employee during the HR implementation at the operational level is likely to trigger different attribution processes regarding the purpose of HR practices. Typically, the 'favoured' employee may interpret the HR practices to focus on the positive internal factor (e.g. employee wellbeing and development) or a form of social obligation [60]. For example, line managers may provide informal mentoring to the 'favoured' employees to boost their career success. In turn, 'favoured' employees will reciprocate by providing cover-ups for line managers' unethical behaviours (e.g. utilising the organisation's resources to seek favours or build relationships). This uneven implementation of HR practices is likely to diminish the strategic value of HRM, which is utilising 'the people to meet both the short and long-term vision of organisations. On the hand, when the line manager displays autocratic tendencies (e.g. monitoring) towards a certain the employee in a team, he or she may interpret the goal of the HR practices to focus on the negative internal factor (e.g. productivity) than the positive internal factor (employee wellbeing).

Similar to the above analyses, this variability in causal attribution is dependent on whether the line manager's paternalistic leadership behaviour is distinctive, collectively interpreted by all team members, and consistent across different situations. High distinctiveness will signal to employees that their line manager does not express paternalistic leadership behaviour across a similar situation. Low consensus will show that employees do not collectively agree those line managers' paternalistic dynamics follow the same pattern. Low consistency will reveal that the line manager does not express paternalism consistently over time. In this context, the employee is likely to ascribe the causality for leadership behaviour in the HR implementation process to external factors (e.g. social affiliations). On another note, when there is low distinctiveness, high consensus, and high consistency, employees will ascribe the causality for the leadership behaviour to internal factors (e.g. line manager's HR dispositions). The latter is likely to occur when line managers display paternalistic leadership behaviour (autocratic and benevolence) in a synergetic manner, whereby autocratic leadership behaviour will be interpreted as an HR cue for quantity-focused outcomes while the benevolent side will be ascribed to positive HR cues for the reward for outstanding performance. In Nigeria's cultural context, this attribution pattern is likely to be interpreted as a more prototypical leadership style capable of implementing HR practices for stronger motivational and organisational outcomes.

6. Implications for future HR research

HRM research in the African context has adopted either a content approach [15, 57] or a contextual approach [22, 57] to analyse the effects of HR practices on organisational outcomes. However, not much is known about the process approach to HRM in the African context. Process approach connotes how HR is transmitted to the employees and how employee's perceptions and cognitions of those HR practices influence uniform understanding (the HR strength) and execution of HR goals [48]. Scholars have reported that the employee HR process is crucial in determining the effectiveness of HR practices to predict positive outcomes [60, 61]. Specifically, employees' perception and interpretation of implemented HR practices are more salient to positive employee attitudes, behaviour, and organisational outcomes than intended HR practices (e.g. content HR approach) [9]. This is because employees, as the final 'consumer' of practices, are responsible for translating HR strategy, policies, and practices into tangible outcomes.

As such, the first implication of this review for future HRM research in Africa is adopting process theories such as attribution theories to examine the employee's cognition of HR practices. Pursuing such research will contribute to the theory development of HRM in the African context as well as uncover the roles of employees' cognitive processes in the evaluation of Western-developed HRM in the African context. For example, scholars might gain particularistic cues (e.g. employees) needed for designing contextualised HRM policies and practices capable of yielding positive organisational outcomes in a disparate national context. To achieve this, I suggest integrating the three main attribution theories to capture broader cognitive complexities that influence employees' HR attribution process. Moreover, future longitudinal HRM research could investigate whether and how employee HR attributions may change over time in the African context. This may be due to a change in HR strategy and policies, government regulations, social exchange at work, line manager's leadership behaviour, etc. Conducting this research is likely to help gain a better understanding of the HR attribution process as an unbounded cognitive process based on the informational resources at the employee's disposal at a time [43].

Secondly, there is a lack of research on the role of line managers' leadership behaviour in the HR implementation process in the African context. As already stated, the concept of leadership in Africa is rooted in paternalism [57], a dynamic mix of benevolent and authoritarian leadership styles. Based on the ethnic, social, and religious diversity of Nigeria context, the line manager can display differentiated paternalistic leadership behaviour in the HR implementation process. As such, future research might benefit from this review by investigating the possibility of differentiated paternalism in the HRM process in the Nigerian context. One way to conduct this research is to examine the links between differentiated paternalistic leadership to employee perception of fairness in the HR implementation process. There is also an opportunity to examine whether differentiated paternalism accounted for differences in leader-member exchange within a team while accounting for the variances in ethnicity etc. Conducting this research is likely to contribute to leadership development programs with a focus on the enactment of HR practice at the operational level.

Third, there is a lack of research on employees' HR attribution across the private and public sector organisations. Public sector organisations possess certain defining features, such as standardised employment practices, collectivised labour unions, etc. that differentiate them from the private sector organisations - the latter is characterised by profit maximisation, selective HR practices, and private ownership. Based on Kelly's covariation model, future research might benefit from this review by investigating the type of information pattern (distinctiveness, consensus, and consistency) used by employees in making casual attribution about HR practices in both public and private sector organisations. Such the examination is likely to help detect the factors (e.g. organisational structure) that influences employee HR attribution in both organisational settings.

7. Limitation of this review

The first limitation of this review is the lack of empirical data to test the assumptions of HR attribution theories in the Nigerian context. Empirical data could provide a researcher with actionable evidence needed for evaluating the HR context for better motivational and organisational outcomes. To conduct this research and due to the nascent stage of HR process research in the Nigeria context, I suggest integrating both qualitative and quantitative research methods (mixed method). This will

DOI: http://dx.doi.org/10.5772/intechopen.110321

help to develop rich and broader insights about the nature of HR practices in the Nigerian context. Specifically, research may first adopt a qualitative research method (e.g. interview or focus group) to understand the HRM context and other emergent themes that could guide subsequent data collection. Then, supplement it with the quantitative method to formulate generalisable explanations about HR attributions to the wider organisation's population in Nigeria. The second limitation is the lack of consideration for individual difference factors that may affect the employee HR attribution process. Hewett et al. [10] suggested that employee HR attribution is likely to be shaped by their values, personalities, goals, needs, social roles, and identities, as well as their past experiences, competencies, and expectancies. Considering these individual factors is likely to explain employees' attributional process beyond the socio-cultural and economic contextual issues raised in this review. As such, future research might benefit from a study that considers individual factor variables alongside contextual factors to capture the multilevel factors affecting employee HR attribution in the Nigerian context. Lastly, this review considered only a singular HR practice (recruitment and selection) at the department level and the line manager's leadership behaviour at the operational level. As such, there is an opportunity to consider other HR practices such as employee involvement at both department and operational levels. Differences in an employee's perception of involvement may influence how they make sense of their organisation's HR practices. Research could also examine whether an employee's perception of involvement at the department level or their perception of involvement at the operation level matters more in the HR attribution process. This will help diagnose whether general HR practices are more important to HR attribution or the discretionary HR practices at the operational level.

In addition, there is also a tendency for an employee to interpret particular HR practices differently from other HR practices. For example, a particular HR practice (e.g. pay and rewards) that fulfils an employee's personal needs and goals might be interpreted more positively than other HR practices (employee involvement). Such an HR attribution process may be present in the Nigerian context where there is a cultural expectation for organisational control and lower employee involvement than in the Western context. Moreover, the poor economic conditions in Nigeria means that employee may prioritise monetary rewards (extrinsic factors) over employment involvement (intrinsic factors). As such, research may consider examining different HR attribution processes across different HR practices. This will help the organisation streamline its resources to crucial motivational mechanisms in the organisation.

8. Conclusion

The one-size-fits-all rationale of western-developed HR practices has been criticised to overlook the particularities of the local business environment. More importantly, it failed to consider the role of people's cognition of HR practices in disparate contexts. In this chapter, I reviewed the contextual factors and the implied meanings of HR practices in Nigeria. I evaluated different attribution patterns that may be at play among employees in the country based on their social and ethnic affiliations as well as the influence of line managers' paternalism in the HR attributional process. Based on the analyses, I suggested that implementing a contextually fit HRM might trigger unique causal attributions among employees, which could have implications for their motivation, behaviour, and performance.

Author details

Paul Nwanna
Centre for Decent Work, Institute for Work Psychology, University of Sheffield, Sheffield, England

*Address all correspondence to: penwanna1@sheffield.ac.uk

References

[1] Latukha M, Poor S, Mitskevich E, Linge D. Human resource management practices transferring from foreign firms to Russia: The case of MNCs subsidiaries. Journal of Business Research. 2020;**108**:476-486

[2] Oppong NY. Human resource management transfer challenges within multinational firms: From tension to best-fit. Management Research Review. 2018;**41**(7):860-877

[3] Aksom H, Zhylinska O, Gaidai T. Can institutional theory be refuted, replaced, or modified? International Journal of Organizational Analysis. 2020;**28**(1):135-159

[4] Farndale E, Paauwe J. SHRM and context: Why firms want to be as different as legitimately possible. Journal of Organizational Effectiveness: People and Performance. 2018;**5**(3):202-210

[5] Wood G, Bischoff C. Human resource management in Africa: Current research and future directions—Evidence from South Africa and across the continent. The International Journal of Human Resource Management. 2022;*33*(3):444-471

[6] Nwagbara U. Exploring how institutions shape managerial employment relations and work-life balance (WLB) challenges in Nigeria. Employee Relations. 2020;**42**(6):1401-1421

[7] Opute JE. HRM in Africa. London: Palgrave Macmillan, Cham; 2020

[8] Oseghale RO, Pepple D, Ifere SE, Amaugo AN. Organization culture types and the replication of transferred human resource management practices in multinational subsidiaries in Nigeria. Employee Relations. 2022:44

[9] Sanders K, Guest D, Rodrigues R. The role of HR attributions in the HRM–outcome relationship: Introduction to the special issue. Human Resource Management Journal. 2021;**31**:694-703

[10] Hewett R, Shantz A, Mundy J, Alfes K. Attribution theories in human resource management research: A review and research agenda. International Journal of Human Resource Management. 2017;**29**:1-40

[11] Heider F. The Psychology of Interpersonal Relations. New York: Wiley; 1958

[12] Kelley HH. The processes of causal attribution. American Psychologist. 1973;**28**(2):107-128

[13] Weiner B. Reflections on the history of attribution theory and research: People, personalities, publications, problems. Social Psychology. 2008;**39**:151-156

[14] Okoli CI, Okeke SI. Extent of strategy human resource management practices adopted by owners of SMEs for business success in Anambra state, Nigeria. European Journal of Human Resource Management Studies. 2018;*1*(2):121-129

[15] Oruh ES, Dibia C. Employee stress and the implication of high-power distance culture: Empirical evidence from Nigeria's employment terrain. Employee Relations. 2020;**42**(6):1381-1400

[16] Bos-Nehles AC, van Riemsdijk MJ, Kok I, Looise JC. Implementing human resource management successfully: The role of first-line managers. Management Revue. 2006;**17**(3):256-273

[17] Guest D. The role of line managers in the HRM process. In: Sanders K, Yang H,

Patel C, editors. HR Process Research. Cheltenham, UK; Northampton, MA, USA: Edward Elgar; 2021. pp. 178-194

[18] The World Bank Annual Report. Nigeria Development Update. Washington, D.C.: World Bank Group; 2021

[19] The Central Bank of Nigeria. Central Bank of Nigeria Economic Report. Third Quarter. Abuja, Nigeria: The Central Bank of Nigeria; 2021

[20] Akinola AO. Economic reforms in Africa: A critical appraisal. In: Oloruntoba SO, Falola T, editors. The Palgrave Handbook of African Political Economy. Palgrave Handbooks in IPE. Cham: Palgrave Macmillan; 2020

[21] UNCTAD. United Nations Conference on Trade and Development. New York: World Investment Report; 2021

[22] Ikyanyon D, Johnson P, Dawson J. Institutional context and human resource management in Nigeria. Employee Relations. 2020;**42**:1-18

[23] Anakwe U. Human resource management practices in Nigeria: Challenges and insights. International Journal of Human Resource Management. 2002;**13**(7):1042-1059

[24] Dowling PJ. Completing the puzzle: Issues in the development of the field of international human resource management. Management International Review. 1999;**39**:27-44

[25] Eisenstadt SN. Tradition, Chandge and Modernity. New York: Wiley; 1973

[26] Akwei C, Nwachukwu C. An exploration of contextual factors affecting the nexus of competitive strategy and human resource management practices in Nigeria emerging economy context. The International Journal of Human Resource Management. 2022:1-44

[27] Ogbewere BI. Governance crises in developing countries: Theoretical and empirical perspectives to Nigeria's public sector. International Journal of Public Administration. 2020;**43**(16):1376-1385

[28] National Bureau of Statistics. Labor force statistics vol. 1: Unemployment and Underemployment Report (Q3-Q4 2022). Abuja: NBS; 2022

[29] Gbadpmosi G, Adisa TA. Human resource Management in Nigeria. A review and conceptual model. In: Adisa TA, Mordi C, editors. Human Resource Management in the Global South: A Critical Perspective. Cham, London: Palgrave Macmillan; 2022. pp. 17-52

[30] Nnoli O. Ethnicity and Development in Nigeria. Aldershot, England: Avebury for United Nations Research Institute for Social Development (UNRISD); 1995

[31] Barney JB. Firm resources and sustained competitive advantage. Journal of Management. 1991;**17**:99-120

[32] Arthur W, Woehr DJ, Akande A, Strong MH. Human resource Management in West Africa: Practices and perception. International Journal of Human Management. 1995;**6**:347-367

[33] Debrah YA. Human Resource Management in Ghana. In: Budhwar PS, Debrah YA, editors. Human Resource Management in Developing Countries. London: Routledge; 2001. pp. 190-208

[34] Hofstede G. Culture's Consequences: International Differences in Work-Related Values. Beverly Hills, CA: Sage; 1980

[35] Iyiola AT, Olatoye OA, Oyekanmi TT. Impact of performance appraisal strategy on employee productivity: Evidence

from selected Nigerian banks. Journal of Management and Social Sciences. Jimoh; 2020;**9**(1):770-783

[36] Ovadje, F. and Ankomah, A., (2001). Human resource management in Nigeria. In Budhwar, P.S., Debrah, Y. A, Human Resource Management in Developing Countries. London: Routledge Research, 174-189

[37] First Bank Nigeria: Annual Report. Lagos, Nigeria. 2020

[38] United Nations Development Programme (UNDP). Human development data. Nigeria: UNDP; 2021

[39] Ekekwe N. A Nigeria model for Capitalism. Harvard Business Review: Business and Society; 2021

[40] Jimoh AO, Danlami SA. Strategic human resource management and organisational performance in the Nigerian manufacturing sector: An empirical investigation. International Journal of Business and Management. 2001;**6**(9):46-56

[41] Abdul-Kahar A. Modern challenges of human resource management practice in job placement and recruitment within organisations in the African continent. Journal of Human Resource Management. 2020;**8**(2):69-75

[42] Igwesi-Chidobe CN, Anyaene C, Akinfeleye A, Anikwe E, Gosselink R. Experiences of physiotherapists involved in front-line management of patients with COVID-19 in Nigeria: A qualitative study. BMJ Open. 2022;**12**:e060012

[43] Martinko MJ, Harvey P, Douglas SC. The role, function, and contribution of attribution theory to leadership: A review. The Leadership Quarterly. 2007;**18**(6):561-585

[44] Dong W, Zhong L. How and when responsible leadership facilitates work engagement: A moderated mediation model. Journal of Managerial Psychology. 2022;**37**(6):545-558

[45] Yelderman LA, Lawrence TI, Lyons CE, DeVault A. Actor–observer asymmetry in perceptions of parole board release decisions. Psychiatry, Psychology and Law. 2021;**28**(5):623

[46] Allen MS, Robson DA, Martin LJ, Laborde S. Systematic review and meta-analysis of self-serving attribution biases in the competitive context of organized sport. Personality and Social Psychology Bulletin. 2020;**46**(7):1027-1043

[47] Fiske ST, Taylor SE. Social Cognition. 2nd ed. New York: McGraw-Hill; 1991

[48] Bowen DE, Ostroff C. Understanding HRM-firm performance linkages: The role of the "strength" of the HRM system. Academy of Management Review. Debrah; 2004;**29**(2):203-221

[49] Mischel W. Toward a cognitive social learning reconceptualization of personality. Psychological Review. 1973;**80**:252-283

[50] Nishii LH, Lepak DP, Schneider B. Employee attributions of the "why" of HR practices: Their effects on employee attitudes and behaviours, and customer satisfaction. Personnel Psychology. 2008;**31**(3):503-545

[51] Ukeje IO, Ndukwe C, Emma C, Ogbulu U, Onele JC. Public service recruitment practices and implications for sustainable development in Ebonyi state, Nigeria. International Journal of Public Administration. National Bureau of Statistics. 2020;**43**(4):361-372

[52] Budwar PS, Debrah YA. Human Resource Management in Developing Countries. London: Routledge; 2001. pp. 1-15

[53] Olugbile F. Nigeria at Work (a Survey of the Psychology of Work among Nigerians). Lagos, Nigeria: Malthouse Press Limited; 1997

[54] Alford J, Greve C. Strategy in the public and private sectors: Similarities, differences, and changes. Administrative Sciences. 2017;7(4):35

[55] Guest D, Sanders K, Rodrigues R, Oliveira T. Signally theory as a framework for analysing HRM processes and integrating HR attribution theories: A conceptual and empirical analysis. Human Resource Management Journal. 2020;**31**:796-818

[56] House RJ, Hanges PJ, Javidan M, Dorfman PW, Gupta V. Culture, Leadership, and Organisations. The Globe Study of 62 Societies. United Kingdom: Sage Publications; 2004

[57] Okereke C, Vincent O, Mordi C. Determinants of Nigerian managers' environmental attitude: Africa's Ubuntu ethics versus global capitalism. Thunderbird International Business Review. 2018;**60**(4):577-590

[58] Farh J, Cheng B. A cultural analysis of paternalistic leadership in Chinese organizations. In: Tsui AS, Li JT, editors. Management and Organizations in the Chinese Context. London: Macmillan; 2000. pp. 84-127

[59] Townsend K, Wilkinson A, Allan C, Bamber G. Mixed signals in HRM: The HRM role of hospital line managers. Human Resource Management Journal. Mischel; 2011;**22**:267-282

[60] Xian HP, Atkinson C, Meng-Lewis Y. Guanxi and high-performance work system: Evidence from a Chinese state-owned Enterprise. International Journal of Human Resource Management. 2017;**30**(19):2685-2704

[61] Alfes K, Veld M, Furstenberg N. The relationship between perceived high-performance work systems, combinations of human resource well-being, and human resource performance attributions. Human Resource Management Journal. 2020;**3**(31):729-752

Chapter 6

Challenges and Opportunities to Internationalize the Indonesian Higher Education Sector

Linda Lambey, Elni Jeini Usoh, Robert Lambey and John Burgess

Abstract

The higher education (HE) system in Indonesia is complex and fragmented, with 4.5 thousand universities offering over 25 thousand majors. The system includes public and private universities, institutes, schools of higher learning, academies, community colleges, and polytechnics. Despite growth in institutions and enrolments, the country's higher education institutions rank low across global rating indicators. The major weaknesses within the higher education sector include the absence of consistent academic quality standards, inconsistent certification, accreditation, supervision, and monitoring processes, an absence of postgraduate-trained staff, and limited research output in recognized international journals. Programs are not linked to workforce skill requirements and graduate unemployment and underemployment rates are high. The word "Internationalization" for Indonesian higher education practically means to "go international" in every aspect of higher education including its education quality and standards, staffing, research, and graduates. The Indonesian government has given priority to the internationalization of universities that includes the goal that universities improve their competitiveness and quality so that they effectively compete globally for staff, students, and research funding. To internationalize, Indonesian universities will have to improve quality across staffing, programs, teaching, and research.

Keywords: higher education, Indonesia, internationalization, quality of education, world-class universities

1. Introduction

The services sector is being globalized through such processes as outsourcing and international consolidation. The services sector accounts for a growing share of output and jobs across the OECD [1]. At the same time, international trade and investment in the services sector have increased [1]. Global corporations dominate service industries such as accounting, the media, publishing, finance, communications, and logistics. As a service industry education is also undergoing a process of globalization. In the higher education sector, there are universities with global reputations (Harvard, MIT, Cambridge, Oxford) and multinational publishing houses that provide integrated courses to universities and students globally and dominate the publishing of academic journals. The process of globalization is supported by technological developments associated with the Fourth Industrial Revolution that "*concerns the digital transformation in society and business - an interface between technologies in the physical, digital and biological disciplines....Emerging technology such as artificial intelligence, robotics, the Internet of Things, autonomous vehicles, 3-D printing, nanotechnology, biotechnology, materials science, energy storage, and quantum computing, represent just the tip of this technology iceberg" ([2]*, 2). Globalized universities can have a local presence, without a physical campus, *via* online courses. Enrolments in online learning programs are expanding exponentially, placing pressure on traditional university systems [3]. In the age of the Fourth Industrial Revolution, globalization is occurring without being accompanied by foreign direct investment and presence in the countries from which students are enrolled. In addition, technology is transforming teaching and learning processes and supporting sophisticated research programs *via* such processes as artificial intelligence, cloud data storage, big data analysis, biotechnology, and machine learning [2].

In this chapter, the discussion is on internationalization, a separate, but related process to globalization. The focus of internationalization is on developing an international component into these core functions—teaching, research, and engagement. Globalization refers to trade, investment, and integration of the sector across countries and has an industry focus. With respect to the higher education (HE), sector internationalization encompasses many dimensions and processes. These include the curriculum, students, staff, research, governance, and reputation. Within this chapter, the nature of internationalization in the context of the Indonesian HE system is mapped and the opportunities and challenges to internationalizing the sector are discussed. As with other emerging economies, there is a national goal to increase access to education and to develop human capability through increased participation in post-secondary education [4]. This is a global aspirational goal linked to improving living standards and the quality of life [5]. To pursue this process requires a HE sector that provides access to those seeking post-secondary education, relevant programs that are linked to national and personal goals, and quality education that ensures graduate employability and supports growth and productivity [6]. To this end, internationalization is a process in HE that supports the qualitative improvement in programs and contributes to broader national and personal development objectives.

For all countries, investment and quality higher education systems are important as they contribute to human capital development, the alleviation of poverty, the productivity of industry, innovation, and development, and core skill development [7]. For individuals and nations, the returns from investment in the HE sector are significant [7]. Investing in HE remains an important step toward achieving many development goals:

> *Economic research unequivocally illustrates high private and social rates of return for investments in tertiary education, including research. The benefits include higher employment and earnings, productivity growth and innovation, greater social stability, more effective public sector bureaucracies, increased civic engagement, and better health outcomes. The consequences of underinvestment in tertiary education include talent loss, limited access to applied research capacity for local problem solving, hindered economic growth due to low levels of skills in the workforce,*

> *low-quality teaching and learning at every level of education, and, perhaps most glaringly, expanded wealth inequality both within countries and among nations, with those investing proportionately more experiencing more innovation and attraction of investment. ([7], p. 2).*

Making progress toward the UN sustainable development goals, especially reducing poverty, improving living standards, and improving equity requires a significant investment in HE [8]. For this reason, it is important for a country like Indonesia to not only invest in the HE sector but ensure that the sector is efficient and effective [9]. To this end, examining internationalization is an important part of supporting the qualitative development of the HE sector.

In this chapter the internationalization of the Indonesian HE sector is evaluated in terms of the progress toward internationalization, the barriers faced, and the programs and policies in place to support internationalization. To address these issues, the chapter draws on secondary sources through academic literature and from reports by national and international agencies. The chapter is organized as follows. First, an outline of the Indonesia HE sector is provided. Then, there follows an examination of the process of internationalization of the HE sector. Following is a discussion of the evidence on the standing and progress toward internationalization of the Indonesian HE sector. The challenges for realizing internationalization in Indonesia are outlined. This is followed by an assessment of current programs to support internationalization. Finally, the chapter reflects on the key processes that are required to support the internationalization of the Indonesian HE sector.

2. Background to Indonesia

Indonesia has over 18 thousand islands. The Indonesian economy, politics, population, and education system are concentrated in Java and Sumatra. Over 85 percent of Indonesia's GDP is generated from these locations [10]. As in nearly all emerging economies, there is a national program toward improving living standards, increasing employment opportunities, and developing globally competitive industries. With sustained GDP growth, increased education participation, a shift away from agriculture, and migration to urban areas, the share of those in poverty has declined over the past two decades [11]. There has been an ongoing emigration of Indonesia workers to Asia and the Middle East working in hospitality, domestic work, construction, and plantations [10]. Indonesia has had to deal with natural disasters including earthquakes, tsunamis, fires, floods, and volcanic eruptions. The economy was hit hard by the Asian financial crisis (1997–1998), the global financial crisis (2008–2009), periodic fluctuations in world oil prices, and the COVID-19 pandemic [12].

Indonesia has the largest population and economy in SE Asia. Indonesia's economy has moved from being the world's 27th largest economy in 2000 to the 16th largest in 2018 [11]. There are many ethnic groups, the dominant ones being Javanese and Sundanese. The main religion of Indonesia is Islam, and this plays an important role in Indonesian culture and politics. The structure of the Indonesian economy shifted from dependence on agriculture in the 1950s and 1960s to industrialization and urbanization from the late [13]. Indonesia's GDP composition by sector share is agriculture (0.14), industry (O.41), and services (0.45) [14]. The major exports of Indonesia were processed and unprocessed commodities including palm oil, coal briquettes, petroleum gas, crude petroleum, and rubber [15].

A feature of the economy is the large share of informal or unregulated employment, especially in agriculture. There are high rates of youth unemployment and underemployment throughout the economy, and the female labor force participation rate is well below that of males [15, 16]. Despite the ongoing structural change, per capita income growth is low, and poverty is widespread [17]. Productivity growth has been limited, reflecting low rates of investment, especially in skills, and labor-intensive production, especially in agriculture [15]. While the formal sector has expanded, the informal sector remains large and many jobs in the formal sector are short term and insecure [10, 18]. Contributing to low productivity growth are the limited and dated infrastructure and unreliable electricity supplies [13].

Despite the expansion in secondary and HE education and participation in Indonesia, there has been an ongoing skills gap and graduate employability problem. Pryono and Nankervis [19] reported that key skills gaps across occupations included senior managers and professionals, scientists, and engineers, and major skills shortages across several industry sectors that included agriculture, forestry, hunting and fishing, transport and storage, finance, insurance, real estate, and business services. Despite the record enrolments in HE, the skill shortages were persistent, especially in the professions [19].

While Indonesia reported GDP growth of 5 percent over the last decade, employment growth has been one percent or less on average [17]. In part, this reflects the large informal and unregulated employment sector that accounts for about three-quarters of the workforce. GDP growth does not translate into formal job growth. In addition, there have traditionally been high rates of youth unemployment and underemployment, and the female labor force participation rate is considerably below that of males [15, 16]. Despite GDP growth, per capita income is low, and poverty is widespread [17, 20]. Productivity growth has stalled because of limited investment in skills and training, labor-intensive production, and the large share of irregular employment in the formal sector that results in limited investment in training [15].

Post-COVID, there has been a strong recovery, though the COVID pandemic had a major negative impact on the economy. The IMF [21] review of the Indonesian economy noted that the economy was expected to recover with real GDP growth forecast to be over 5 percent for 2022 and 6 percent for 2022. Despite the predicted strong growth, the IMF [21] identified several risks to ongoing growth, and these included adverse global conditions (increasing inflation and interest rates) and risks from global climate change with Indonesia at risk given its dependence on hydrocarbons, the extensive de-afforestation occurring throughout the archipelago, its location in an active earthquake/volcanic zone, and the risk of severe storms/typhoons.

3. The Indonesian education system

The Indonesian education system is the fourth largest in the world with over 50 million students, 3 million teachers, and 300,000 schools [22]. Pre-school education in Indonesia is not compulsory. There are around 50,000 kindergartens in Indonesia, nearly all of which are privately owned. Children are required to attend 12 years of school. Students can choose among state-run, non-sectarian public schools, and religious schools. There are around 170,000 primary schools, 40,000 junior-secondary schools, and 26,000 high schools. About 84 percent of these schools are under the Ministry of Education and Culture and the remaining 16 percent are under the Ministry of Religious Affairs.

There are two types of high schools in Indonesia: SMA (Sekolah Menengah Atas) and SMK (Sekolah Menengah Kejuruan). SMA students are prepared to continue to higher education, while SMK, as a vocational school, prepares its students to work after finishing their schooling, without moving on to higher education. There are also around 200 international schools in Indonesia. International schools adopt an international curriculum such as IB (International Baccalaureate) or CIE (Cambridge International Examinations) that support English entry qualifications into university programs that are taught in English and offshore [23].

The participation rates in secondary education are high at around 98 percent, but the participation rate in tertiary education is 36 percent [24]. In 2021, around 3.21 million students were enrolled in state universities. State universities are under the purview of the Ministry of Research, Technology, and Higher Education of Indonesia. These universities exclude state universities with religious affiliations that fall under the Ministry of Religion's responsibility [25]. In 2021, there were around three thousand private universities in Indonesia. Private universities in Indonesia operate on budgets that are almost entirely tuition-fee driven, and students get limited, if any, financial support from the government to attend such universities [26].

There has been a concerted push to increase investment and enrolments in the HE sector. The World Bank [4] commented that Indonesia:

> *"has drastically increased investment in the sector and instituted important reforms at all levels of education. This has led to rapid increases in access, especially for the poor and in secondary education. The number of higher education students has doubled in five years. Overall spending for higher education has tripled in real terms, to over 30 trillion rupiah. The plans for further expansion are aggressive. The Governments plans include tripling the number of students in technical programs and increasing the number of doctoral students fivefold by 2025. The new Higher Education Law 12/2012 establishes that each district should have its own community college. Indonesia has also been putting policies in place to continue expanding access to senior secondary and higher education."*

As set out by the government, the strategic objectives of the Indonesia HE sector include the following:

"(1) increased quality of higher education learning and student affairs; (2) increased quality of science and technology institutions and higher education; (3) increased relevance, quality and quantity of science and technology and higher education resources; (4) increased research and development relevance and productivity; and (5) Strengthening innovation capacity [27]."

As of 2021, there are 125 state universities in Indonesia. Entering state universities in Indonesia is arguably harder than private universities as the top Indonesian universities are dominated by state universities. There are three ways to qualify for Indonesian state universities: firstly, by invitation. Students, whose grades in the last five semesters of high school meet the university entrance criteria, would be nominated by their schools to receive an invitation to the universities of their choice. Students who do not receive an invitation to enter state universities could still qualify by either sitting for the nationwide university entrance exams or sitting for an independent entry selection examination offered at selected state universities [25].

The Indonesian education framework is complex and fragmented, and contains many internal contradictions. Within the HE system, there are public and private universities, institutes, schools of higher learning, academies, community colleges, and polytechnics. The key policy challenges for the sector include inconsistent academic quality standards; inconsistent certification, accreditation, supervision, and monitoring techniques; and academics who do not possess post-graduate qualifications and research experience [9, 28]. As with many other countries in the region ([19], 21) there are problems for graduates transitioning to jobs, with most graduates being without full-time employment from four to eight months after graduation, and with many of those in jobs that are unrelated to the professions in which they were educated [29].

4. Graduate work readiness challenges in Indonesia

The high rates of underemployment and problems in accessing the labor market is a persistent problem for Indonesian graduates [19] and points to a longer-term structural failure in the HE system in Indonesia. Reviews of graduates by international agencies found gaps in graduate attributes including critical thinking, communication and independent working competencies, leadership, team orientation, creativity, English-language fluency, and information technology skills [4]. Other work-ready deficiencies identified included personal integrity, intellectual capacity, teamwork, analysis, and problem-solving skills [44]. The OECD [5] identified weaknesses in literacy and numeracy, job flexibility, work sequencing, time management, and team working abilities. The literature review by Priyono and Nankervis [19] revealed that there is a growing mismatch between the skill and job demands of industry and the attributes and capabilities of new graduates. As a result graduate unemployment and underemployment exist alongside national skills shortages. In their review, Priyono and Nankervis [19] indicated that the graduate work skills gap was not confined to the problems of curriculum and education, but reflected an overall failure of integration and coordination between government ministries associated with education, employment, skills, and training; the weak communication processes across the key stakeholders, including industry, education, and national and provincial governments; and the need for greater flexibility, increased funding of training and education, and innovative pedagogies in educational institutions. The World Bank [4] identified the mismatch between program enrolments and the changing structure of the economy. The two largest programs were public administration and teaching, both linked to scholarship access; but the shares were out of line with the occupational composition of the economy.

The World Bank [4] commented further:

> *"A certain degree of difficulty in finding qualified workers may be a sign of a healthy economy. As new and more evolved technologies are used (broadly defined to include not only physical production but also service provision), one expects employers to have a hard time finding workers who are ready for the new technologies. However, it may also be a sign that the education sector is not providing graduates with the right skills. The level of unemployment faced by higher education graduates, which is stubbornly high until the age of 35, maybe a sign of the latter. As the system expands so rapidly, it is important to ensure that the sector is preparing graduates for the labor market."*

Addressing graduate work readiness challenges cannot be the sole responsibility of universities; however, they do have a responsibility to graduates and the broader community to support an effective and fast transition into employment for those occupations for which graduates were educated. Internationalization is one component of meeting this challenge since it embodies many of the necessary attributes that improve graduate employability. These attributes include having soft skills that include a world view, tolerance, multiculturalism, effective communication, and cross-cultural engagement [19].

5. International performance indicators linked to education

The need for an institution of higher education to attain the status of a world-class university is an important objective for many universities in Indonesia. The Indonesian government has emphasized the need for the internationalization of universities through the 2003–2010 Higher Education Long-Term Strategy (HELTS), which declared that universities in Indonesia were expected to significantly improve their competitiveness and quality so that they could compete globally [49]. Following the HELTS 2003–2010, the Directorate General of Higher Education outlined HELTS for the period from 2011 through 2020, which focuses on integrating internal and external quality assurance and developing a higher education institutions database [30]. The status of a world-class university will bring benefits and a prestigious impression to the university, but there will be many challenges that must be faced to attain world-class status recognition. It is noted that Indonesian universities need to improve quality and undertake reforms pertaining to matters such as funding, policy, institutional and academic quality, and access to get a better position at the regional and global levels [6].

There are a range of ranking systems to assess universities. These include Shanghai Jia Tong University Rankings, Times Higher Education Supplement (THES), Webometrics Ranking of World Universities, International Rankings Expert Group & The Berlin Principles, Global University City Index, World Education News & Reviews (WENR), Academic Ranking of World Universities, and QS World University Ranking. The purpose of the rankings system is to inform universities, governments, graduates, employers, and prospective students about the standing of a university internationally according to pre-set criteria [31]. The rankings system in general has a Western bias and is predominantly used to rank universities in advanced economies and are used to highlight reputational standing and support brand marketing [32]. The rankings can be gamed and there are critiques of the methodology and applications of the systems [33].

For Indonesia, nine universities are ranked as world-class universities according to QS World: Universitas Indonesia (UI), Institut Teknologi Bandung (ITB), Universitas Gajah Mada (UGM), Universitas Padjajaran, Institut Pertanian Bogor (IPB), Universitas Airlangga (UNAIR), Universitas Diponegoro (UNDIP), Institut Teknologi Sepuluh November (ITS), and Universitas Brawijaya (UB) [34]. Apart from the inherent biases of the world rankings system, they are based on individual universities and do not incorporate the total tertiary education system or the entire education system.

There are indicators of the internationalization of universities. The universities with the largest numbers and shares of international students are found in the USA. The Times Higher Education World University Rankings ranks universities by their globalization through a review of rankings for students and staff by internationalization, international co-authorship of publications, and international reputation metrics. In 2022, the highest ranked universities according to the internationalization criteria were the University of Hong Kong; ETH Zurich; Ecole Polytechnic Federale de Lausanne; and the University of Oxford [35]. Indonesian universities were not listed in these rankings.

The OECD [36] provides a benchmarking assessment of 15-year-old students proficiencies in reading, mathematics, and science. From the 2108 report, Indonesian students scored below the OECD average in reading, mathematics, and science. A smaller proportion than the average of Indonesian students performed at the highest levels of proficiency in at least one subject; at the same time a smaller proportion of students achieved a minimum level of proficiency in at least one subject [36]. Despite these results, the OECD noted that the results had remained constant over the last decade in which there had been a major expansion in school enrolments.

The UN and the World Bank provide system evaluation of education and economic performance. The Human Development Index (HDI) assesses a country's development trajectory using measures of life expectancy, schooling, and GNI per capita, as compared to other countries. For Indonesia, the HDI value was 0.694, in 2017 and it was ranked 116 out of 189 countries. The HDI for Indonesia increased from 0.528 in 1990 to 0.694 in 2017. On all measures of human development, Indonesia improved. The key measures are life expectancy, mean years of schooling and expected years of schooling, and GNI per capita increase [8]. The HDI for Indonesia suggests from 1990 to 2017 that well-being has improved as life expectancy (better health), schooling (education and opportunity), and material well-being (GNI per capita) have improved. The education system has contributed to this improvement, but the education measure applied is schooling based.

The Human Capital Index [37] indicates the extent to which a child who reaches 18 years of age accesses human capital in terms of health and education. It is an indicator of the future productivity of the workforce. In 2018, Indonesia ranks 87 out of 157 countries and ranks low within Southeast Asia and low relative to its income. The HCI score was 0.53, indicating that children who reach 18 years of age only access 53 percent of potential human capital. This suggests a problem with the availability and quality of schooling. For Indonesia, life expectancy and health have improved, as has the HCI ex score. Between 2012 and 017, the HCI score for Indonesia only increased from 0.50 to 0.53 [37].

The Gender Equity Index (GEI) from the World Economic Forum [38] measures gender-based disparities across a range of criteria. The GEI examines national gender gaps for economic, political, education, and health criteria. Indonesia was 95th out of 136 countries in 2013 and its ranking declined from 68th in 2006 to 95th in 2013. The overall disparity for women was around two-thirds of that for men in terms of labor force participation, health, education, and empowerment. The four areas that constitute the index are economic participation and opportunity, health and survival, education attainment, and political empowerment. For the GEI, the challenges are found across all the criteria. For education, women have comparable participation rates to men in schooling, but their participation falls behind in post-secondary education [15]. There are structural barriers that females face in participating in HE and in transitioning into formal sector jobs, this is especially so in rural areas where there are infrastructure shortages and the demands of supporting families and rural enterprises [16].

Indonesian universities do not rank globally according to the different world ranking systems. While different criteria are used across the ranking systems, Indonesian universities, with a few exceptions, are not included in any of the global ranking systems. When reviewing the education system there are several challenges revealed in the systems evaluations outlined above. These include relatively low rates of participation in post-secondary education, the capabilities of students in core competencies, questions around the quality of the education system, and equity and opportunity in the system, especially for females in post-secondary education. For individual universities, the challenge is to improve the quality of staff and programs, improve access for females, and better match jobs with graduates [19]. Within this set of challenges, the internationalization of the HE sector has an important role to play in addressing these objectives.

6. What is the internationalization of higher education?

Internationalization differs from globalization, but they have linked processes. Internationalization of higher education is a process of integrating international/intercultural elements across all elements of a university's operations including teaching, research, service functions, and community engagement [9]. Gao [39] suggests that there are six dimensions of internationalization. For each dimension, there are several indicators. The six dimensions with example indicators are research (number and share of international researchers); students (number and share of international students); staff (number and share with international credentials); curriculum (joint degree programs with international universities); governance (international presence on- and offshore); and engagement (international networks and partnerships).

Internationalization is a response to the impact and processes of globalization, where the HE sector responds to the globalization of the economy, the society, and the labor market through systematic programs that aim to incorporate internationalization into all the key university processes [9]. Internationalization can benefit universities by improving national and international recognition, developing strategic partnerships, expanding academic networks, generating knowledge, improving learning outcomes, increasing research output and quality, and leading to national and international funding opportunities. Internationalization can integrate higher education systems into a global framework, produce graduates with a global vision and multicultural skills, improve the international exchange of staff and students, and build global partnerships [9].

Internationalization not only contributes to enhanced global recognition and standing, but it also supports the core functions of universities. There are multiple manifestations of internationalization that include having staff with international qualifications, publishing in international peer-reviewed journals, having international research partnerships, developing international staff and student exchanges, developing teaching, and learning processes that include international and multicultural elements, recruiting international students and engaging with alumni who are internationally based. Internationalization can potentially permeate through all functions of a university.

The process of internationalization requires a national approach to supporting partnerships with international universities, attracting international students and staff, becoming integrated into regional university networks, establishing research and university hubs, supporting the upgrading of staff qualifications, and "internationalizing" the curriculum [28, 40]. Leadership and investment nationally can support a process that gradually transforms the HE sector toward internationalization.

The Directorate General of Higher Education for Indonesia has emphasized the need for university internationalization through the Long-Term Strategy of Higher Education in 2003–2010 that indicated that universities were expected to improve competitiveness and quality so that they can compete globally [9]. This, in turn, is supported by a national program to establish minimum standards across the sector that include standards for content, processes, staff, infrastructure, management, financing, and program assessment [41].

For Indonesia, internationalization of the university sector is in its infancy. The university rating systems reveal that Indonesian universities have comparatively low rates of publication, especially in peer-reviewed journals. There are few staff with international post-graduate qualifications and there are few international students studying in Indonesia. Indonesia had 53,604 students studying abroad according to UNESCO [23]. The top three destinations were Australia, Malaysia, and the USA. International student enrolments in Indonesia have risen steadily to 7700 students, representing less than one percent of tertiary students in 2018. The largest share of foreign tertiary students studying in Indonesia comes from Myanmar. To date, there is one foreign university operating in Indonesia, Monash University from Australia, which opened a campus in 2022 [42].

7. The challenges facing university internationalization in Indonesia

While Indonesia is a member of ASEAN, there is very limited engagement by Indonesian universities within the region. While many students from Indonesia study abroad, there are few international students within Indonesia. The literature identifies the following challenges for Indonesia that must be addressed if internationalization is to be developed across the HE sectors. There is a lack of coordination and integration across the HE sectors and between key stakeholders in the system. Challenges include improving coordination between the national and provincial government; and between HE institutions, government, and employers [19]. There has also been an absence of a national program to support internationalization, although internationalization is proclaimed as a goal of the HE sector. Although the government has recently announced policies to encourage overseas universities to establish campuses in Indonesia and encourage short-term appointments of academics from overseas universities, there has been limited progress toward realizing these objectives [40]. Institutional conditions, including history, have not supported internationalization. Dutch colonial occupation established a rudimentary education system linked to Colonial ambitions [43]. The current university system meets national and provincial objectives and all the conditions that support internationalization (staffing, students, curriculum, research, reputation) are lacking across the HE system. International campuses are absent, international students are absent, visiting international scholars are absent, and participation in international research projects is minimal. On curriculum and quality of staff and programs, Usoh [9] and Wicaksono and Friawan [44] identified factors impacting quality and the potential for internationalization. These conditions included less government spending on education as compared to countries in the region: the low rates of graduate post-graduate qualifications of Indonesian teaching and lecturing staff; low salaries across the sector; and poor governance of public educational institutions.

Compared to neighbors such as Malaysia, Indonesia has failed to internationalize the HE sector. Malaysia had a national plan supporting internationalization of the sector that included attracting overseas universities, developing international partnerships, establishing university corridor hubs such as the Kuala Lumpur Education City, attracting international staff and international students, and investing in joint industry/university research hubs and facilities [45]. As a result, there are over 100 thousand international students per year and there is an international university presence by universities from North America, Europe, Japan, and Australia/New Zealand [45].

Since 2009 Indonesia's allocated fund for education is 20% of the state budget. However, Indonesian higher education has limited collaboration with private companies, which could invest in education and possibly contribute toward developing a professional and skilled workforce [46–48]. In terms of research, the Ministry of Research, Technology and Higher Education (now Ministry of Education, Culture, Research and Technology) admits that Indonesia has a shortage of active researchers and has the insufficient infrastructure to support science and technology developments and research. It is suggested that given its population size that Indonesia needs 200,000 researchers to support research and development, and research training, there are only 24,000 researchers [47, 49].

University internationalization is slowly emerging in Indonesia when compared to developed countries and with comparable countries in the region such as Malaysia, which have developed an internationalization process in staffing, students, research, and teaching over many decades. State regulations for establishing an International Office in universities were only initiated in 2007. Kyrychenko [47] identifies several barriers to internationalization that include an absence of institutional autonomy and extensive bureaucratic controls and underqualified staff. A further challenge to employability, research development, and internationalization is the lack of English competency across staff and students [18]. Indonesia has low levels of English proficiency as compared to neighboring ASEAN countries such as Malaysia, Singapore, and the Philippines. The application of English as a medium of instruction and research is one of the critical elements for the internationalization of higher education.

Surisno [40] suggested that the barriers to internationalization are systemic and permeate throughout the Indonesia HE system which included the absence of a national unified and extensive policy program to support internationalization, while the government has proclaimed the desire to establish world-class universities in Indonesia, the details and the processes for achieving this goal have not been articulated. At the level of individual universities, Surisno [40] suggested that entrenched and rigid institutional arrangements inhibit innovation, including internationalization, and that university leaders lack the skills or track record to manage innovative programs, including internationalization.

8. Developing a policy program to support internationalization

The Indonesian Ministry of Education Regulation no 26/2007 and Government Regulation number17/2010 have been issued to encourage international cooperation and partnership in the Indonesian higher education sector by establishing the International Office or Office of International Affairs across universities. The function of the international office is to boost all internationalization dimensions from curriculum through to research. To achieve this objective, the first requirement is that there should be a clear case for internationalization. It is not an end but should be recognized for the material and qualitative benefits that are generated for individuals, local communities, and the nation. There is evidence that internationalization supports human capital and social capital development, and in the case of Indonesia contributes to longer-term development goals. Usoh [9] suggested that an internationalization model should include a suite of programs within universities that include:

> *"1) human resources development: the quality improvement of the university's human resources will lead to quality graduates and high employability; 2) research*

development and potential collaboration; 3) skill and labour force; 4) upgrading facilities and infrastructure; 5) training, benchmarking and upgrading staff qualifications; and 6) national and international accreditation improvement."

An internationalization agenda requires that the key stakeholders contribute and cooperate toward the process. The key stakeholders are the central government; regional governments; universities; and industry. Central government must develop and fund an internationalization agenda. It is important for developing the international and national levels of the agenda. This requires objectives, programs, and engagement. At the central level, international universities can be invited and supported to establish regional campuses and partnerships, including international research in trade and investment agreements, international staff can be funded for short-term appointments, and local staff can be funded to attend international universities to receive post-graduate qualifications, and internationalization can be built into funding and quality assurance models governing universities. Surisno [40] argued that the central government should support the establishment of international branch campuses, and especially encourage "leading" international universities to have a presence in Indonesia.

For regional governments, they can coordinate universities to establish international study and research hubs and provide infrastructure for international staff and students. Cooperation across universities can provide opportunities and resources to share visitors, research, and student programs. Indonesia can raise its profile within the region by cooperating across regional institutions and other national higher education systems within ASEAN (Association of South East Asian Nations) and more fully engage with international agencies to improve standards and to accredit the quality of programs [28].

Individual universities can develop programs and the institutional, program, and personal levels to internationalize the curriculum, organize staff and student exchanges internationally, provide scholarships for staff to acquire international qualifications, and sponsor international scholars for short-term appointments [9]. While the capacity and financial capability of universities differs, individual universities can achieve some internationalization. This could be, for example, through programs of student and staff exchanges; sharing international visitors across campuses in the same city; upgrading the curriculum to include international references and topics; upgrading staff qualifications; and participating in international research and teaching programs.

Industry support is required to assist in developing the curriculum and in identifying those attributes that are required to support graduate employability [19], but beyond this industry, engagement is important in funding and developing joint research with universities and with international agencies and international universities. Industry should be actively engaged with teaching and learning processes, but also with research programs, especially where there are opportunities for international collaboration. In turn, the national government can support university hubs and research clusters such as those found in Malaysia to attract international universities, students, staff, and investors [45].

Technological developments are changing all aspects of university teaching and research. Libraries are digitalized and online, and courses can be taught anywhere at any time through online teaching. Curriculum and teaching can be outsourced. Technology has transformed the sector, and the challenge is effectively utilize the technology to support core HE functions. Given the ongoing globalization of the sector, the market for HE is changing. It is not confined to post-school entrants, it is not confined to degree programs, it is not confined to local students, and it is not confined to local face-to-face delivery [3]. The globalization of the sector opens both opportunities and challenges for universities. McKinsey [3] stated that:

> *"From 2011 to 2021, the number of learners reached by massive open online courses (MOOCs) increased from 300,000 to 220 million. Between 2012 and 2019, the number of hybrid and distance-only students4 at traditional universities increased by 36 percent, while the circumstances of the COVID-19 pandemic in 2020 rapidly accelerated that growth by an additional 92 percent".*

McKinsey and Co. [3] went on to comment on the growth in the number of new for-profit providers in the sector in North America that are funded by venture capital. Implicitly, the sector is about to undergo a major structural transformation. For Indonesian universities, the challenge is to adapt and develop the potential of the technologies and to meet the potential global competition from online providers. This will require government and industry support, additional investment in IT and training, and extensive and reliable IT networks.

9. Conclusion

Internationalization of Indonesian universities can address personal and national developmental objectives. There are many elements and dimensions to internationalization. To date, there has been limited internationalization of the Indonesian HE sector. There have been political objections to processes of internationalization, especially involving overseas universities establishing campuses in Indonesia. These may be seen as threats to Indonesian culture and traditions, and agents of cultural imperialism, especially if the institutions were former colonial powers in Asia—the UK, France, and the USA [40]. However, as with other forms of direct foreign investment, Indonesia can impose licensing conditions on foreign university investment and require that universities meet local accreditation and quality standards. Other objections to internationalization could be the costs, the necessity, and the barrier imposed by Bahassa not being an international language of research and learning. On the costs, it is possible for low-cost approaches to be taken to internationalization that are regional and institutional specific, and in accordance with local circumstances [9]. Improving the quality and access to tertiary education are important priorities, and internationalization can be part of these important national programs.

Technological change will globalize the HE sector and offer opportunities and challenges to the sector. Globalization and internationalization do not require traditional processes of direct investment and campus delivery of programs. MOOTs can transform the industry and undermine the local competitive advantage of Indonesian universities. The challenge for universities is sustaining competitive advantage and realizing broader non-commercial objectives such as research and community engagement. Through online delivery, an international program can be created without requiring offshore campuses.

Indonesia can learn from and benchmark off other countries in the region and internationally that have extended international programs and international presence. Malaysia is an example of a neighbor at a similar development stage, with similar natural resources, and similar cultural and language conditions that have internationalized its HE sector. Within the region, wealthier economies such as Singapore, Korea, Japan, and Taiwan have extensive international programs including exchanges, training, collaborative research, and international campuses. China has actively and successfully developed an internationalization agenda for the HE sector that has led to the recognition of several world-class universities [50]. As previously reported, universities in Hong Kong were assessed as being among the most internationalized across the globe [35]. There are many examples of countries at different stages of development, with different histories and cultures, that have been able to successfully achieve some degree of internationalization. Benchmarking can be applied throughout the different levels and stakeholders in the HE sector. Sutrisno [40] suggested that Indonesia can learn from its neighbors, benchmark internationalization programs against countries and universities in the region, and extensively engage and collaborate regionally and internationally.

Author details

Linda Lambey[1], Elni Jeini Usoh[2], Robert Lambey[3] and John Burgess[4*]

1 Organisation Universitas Sam Ratulangi, Manado, Indonesia

2 Universitas Negeri Manado, Indonesia

3 Universitas Sam Ratulangi, Manado, Indonesia

4 Torrens University, Adelaide, South Australia, Australia

*Address all correspondence to: john.burgess@torrens.edu.au

References

[1] OECD. Growth in Services–Fostering Employment, Productivity and Innovation", OECD Digital Economy Papers, No. 94,. Paris: OECD Publishing; 2005. DOI: 10.1787/232370436752

[2] Burgess J, Connell J, Nankervis A, Montague A. Introduction. In: Nankervis A, Connell Montague A, Burgess J, editors. The Fourth Industrial Revolution: What Does it Mean for Australian Industry. Melbourne: Springer Nature; 2021. pp. 1-19

[3] McKinsey and Co. 2022. Demands for Online Education are Growing: Are Providers Ready? Available from: https://www.mckinsey.com/industries/education/our-insights/demand-for-online-education-is-growing-are-providers-ready

[4] World Bank. Indonesia's Higher Education System: How Responsive is it to the Labor Market? 2014. Available from: https://openknowledge.worldbank.org/handle/10986/20017

[5] OECD. Reviews of National Policies for Education: Education in Indonesia. Jakarta: OECD Publishing; 2015

[6] Hill H, Wie T. Education in Indonesia. In: Indonesian Universities: Rapid Growth, Major Challenges. Singapore: Institute of Southeast Asian Studies; 2013

[7] Arnhold N, Basset R. Steering Higher Education: Towards a Resilient System that Delivers for All. World Bank; 2021

[8] United Nations Development Program (UNDP). Human Development Index 2018. New York: UNDP; 2018

[9] Usoh E. The challenging road to world-class university status higher education in eastern Indonesia. In: Dayaram K, Lambey L, Burgess J, Afrianty T, editors. Developing the Workforce in an Emerging Economy: The Case of Indonesia Abingdon. Routledge; 2020. pp. 125-135

[10] Burgess J, Dayaram K, Lambey L, and Afrianty T. The challenges of human resource development in Indonesia. In: Dayaram K, Lambey L, Burgess J, Afrianty T, editors. Developing the Workforce in an Emerging Economy: The Case of Indonesia. Abingdon: Routledge; 2020. pp. 1-17

[11] International Monetary Fund. World Economic Outlook (April 2018). 2018. Available from: http://statisticstimes.com/economy/projected-world-gdp-ranking.php [Accessed: January 18, 2019]

[12] Afrianty T, Artatanaya I, Burgess J. Working from home effectiveness during Covid-19: Evidence from university staff in Indonesia. Asia Pacific Management Review. 2021;**27**(1):50-57

[13] Elias S, Noone C. The Growth and Development of the Indonesian Economy. Reserve Bank of Australia Bulletin; 2011. pp. 33-43

[14] Central Intelligence Agency. The World Fact Book Indonesia. 2019. Available from: https://www.cia.gov/library/publications/resources/the-world-factbook/geos/id.html. [Accessed: January 24, 2019]

[15] Allen E. Analysis of Trends and Challenges in the Indonesian Labour Market. Asian Development Bank Papers on Indonesia. No 16. Jakarta: ADB; 2016

[16] Prihatiningtyastuti E, Dayaram K, Burgess J. Skills development and the challenges for regional

women. In: Dayaram K, Lambey L, Burgess J, Afrianty T, editors. Developing the Workforce in an Emerging Economy: The Case of Indonesia. Abingdon: Routledge; 2020. pp. 53-67

[17] Kudrna G, Le T, Piggott J. Macro-demographics and ageing in emerging Asia: The case of Indonesia. Journal of Population Ageing. 2022;**5**:7-38

[18] Burgess J, Dayaram K, Lambey L, Afrianty T. Addressing human resource development challenges in Indonesia. In: Dayaram K, Lambey L, Burgess J, Afrianty T, editors. Developing the Workforce in an Emerging Economy: The Case of Indonesia. Abingdon: Routledge; 2020. pp. 177-185

[19] Priyono S, Nankervis A. The perfect storm': Constraints on Indonesian economic growth posed by graduate work-readiness challenges. In: Cameron R, Dhakal S, Burgess J, editors. Transitions from Education to Work: Workforce Ready Challenges in the. Asia Pacific, London and New York: Routledge; 2018. pp. 104-124

[20] OECD. Indonesia: Snapshot. Paris: OECD; 2022

[21] IMF. Country Report 22/84, Indonesia. Washington: IMF; 2022

[22] Statista. Education in Indonesia. 2022. Available from: https://www.statista.com/topics/9229/education-in-indonesia/#dossierContents__outerWrapper

[23] International Trade Administration. 2022. Indonesia-Country Commercial Guide. Education and Training. Available from: https://www.trade.gov/country-commercial-guides/indonesia-education-and-training. [Accessed: October 26, 2022]

[24] UNESCO. Indonesia. Paris: Institute for Statistics, UNESCO; 2017

[25] Statista. Number of state university students in Indonesia from 2013 to 2021. 2022. Available from: https://www.statista.com/statistics/704777/number-of-state-university-students-in-indonesia/. [Accessed: October 26, 2022]

[26] Statista. Number of private university students in Indonesia from 2013 to 2021. 2022. Available from: https://www.statista.com/statistics/704753/number-of-private-universities-in-indonesia/. [Accessed: October 26, 2022]

[27] Sudirwan J, Pelawi D. Indonesian higher education learning strategy facing industry 4.0: Program for implementing the SPOCs learning model. In: 2019 International Conference on Information Management and Technology (ICIMTech). Vol. 1. Denpasser: IEEE; 2019. pp. 548-553

[28] Welch A. The limits of regionalism in Indonesian higher education. Asian Education and Development Studies. 2012;**1**(1):24-42

[29] Hoeckel K. Youth labour markets in the early twenty first century. In: Mann A, Stanley J, Archer L, editors. Understanding Employer Engagement in Education: Theories and Evidence. Abingdon, Oxon: Routledge; 2014. pp. 66-76

[30] Iskandar I. Higher education in ASEAN: Working paper in EU Centre intern and NUS political science honours graduate. 2009. Available from: www.eucentre.sg/wpcontent/uploads/2013/06/WorkingPaper-HEAinASEAN-2009-08-01.pdf.

[31] Altbach P. The Costs and Benefits of World-Class Universities. USA: International Higher Education, The Boston College Center for International Higher Education, 5-8, January–February; 2007

[32] Komatar M. Global university rankings and their impact on the internationalisation of higher education. European Journal of Education. 2018;**54**(2):299-310

[33] UNESCO. "Rankings and Accountability in Higher Education: Uses and Misuses." 2016. Available from: https://wayback.archive-it.org/10611/20161117160330/http://www.unesco.org/new/en/education/resources/in-foc us-articles/rankings/)

[34] Harususilo Y. Ini dia 9 universities terbaik di Indonesia. Diunduh dari Harian Kompas. 2018. Available from: https://edukasi.kompas.com/read/2018/06/13/11511331/infografik-ini-dia-9-universitas-terbaik-indonesia-versi-qs-world. [Accessed: Juni 13, 2018]

[35] Times Higher Education (THE). Most International Universities. 2022. Available from: https://www.timeshighereducation.com/student/best-universities/most-international-universities-world

[36] OECD. County Note: Indonesia. 2018. Available from: https://www.oecd.org/pisa/publications/PISA2018_CN_IDN.pdf

[37] World Bank. Human Capital Index. 2019. Available from: https://databank.worldbank.org/reports.aspx?source=3698&series=HD.HCI.EYRS

[38] World Economic Forum. The Global Gender Gap Report. Geneva: WEF; 2015

[39] Gao Y. A set of indicators for measuring and comparing university internationalisation performance across national boundaries. High Education. 2018;**76**:317-336. DOI: 10.1007/s10734-017-0210-5

[40] Sutrisno A. Internationalisation of Indonesian higher education: Recent initiatives and their problems. International Higher Education. 2019;**97**:12-13

[41] Helda & Syaharani. National standards of education in contents standards and education process standards in Indonesia. Indonesian Journal of Education. 2022;**2**(3):257-269

[42] Monash University. Indonesia's First Foreign University Unveiled. 2022. Available from: https://www.monash.edu/news/articles/indonesias-first-first-foreign-university-unveiled. [Accessed: October 26, 2022]

[43] K12 Academics. The History of Education in Indonesia. 2021. Available from: https://www.k12academics.com/Education%20Worldwide/Education%20in%20Indonesia/history-education-indonesia

[44] Wicaksono TY, Friawan D. 8 recent developments in higher education in Indonesia: Issues and challenges. In: Armstrong S, Chapman BJ, editors. Financing Higher Education and Economic Development in East Asia. Canberra: ANU E. Press; 2011. pp. 159-187

[45] Grapragasem S, Krishnan A, Mansor A. Current trends in Malaysian higher education and the effect on education policy and practice: An overview. International Journal of Higher Education. 2014;**3**(1):85-93

[46] Indonesia-Investments. Unemployment rate Indonesia falls to 5.5% of labor force. 2016. Available from: https://www.indonesia-investments.com/news/todays headlines/unemployment-rate-indonesia-falls-to-5.5-of-labor-force/item6788

[47] Kyrychenko V. Indonesia's higher education: Context, policy, and perspective. Asian Journal

of Contemporary Education. 2018;**2**(2):159-172

[48] Statista. Indonesia: Unemployment rate from 2007 to 2017. 2018. Available from: https://www.statista.com/statistics/320129/unemployment-rate-in-indonesia/

[49] Rochim M. The Ministry of Research, Technology and Higher Educations Break through for Research Mechanism in Indonesia. Ministry of Research, Technology and Higher Education of the Republic of Indonesia; 2016

[50] Wang QH, Wang Q, Liu N. Building world-class universities in China: Shanghai Jiao Tong University. In: The Road of Academic Excellent. Washington, DC: The World Bank; 2011. pp. 33-62

Chapter 7

Work-Related Safety and Health Issues among Food and Parcel Delivery Riders

Syazwan Syah Zulkifly

Abstract

The COVID-19 pandemic and advancements in digital technology have led to significant growth in the gig economy's commercial food and parcel delivery sectors. In Malaysia, freelance riders known as P-hailing deliverers prioritize customer ratings and delivery speed over occupational safety and health (OSH), often engaging in risky riding behavior and violating road-traffic regulations. The Royal Malaysia Police reported a twenty-fold increase in accidents involving P-hailing riders in 2020 compared to the previous year. This study aimed to uncover OSH issues among P-hailing riders in Malaysia. A literature review and semi-structured interviews with riders and digital platform representatives were conducted. The findings confirmed that deliverers face numerous hazards, including exposure to unsafe road conditions, reckless road users, extreme temperatures, dust, smoke, unpredictable weather, biological hazards (viruses and bacteria), and vibrations. Additionally, they are vulnerable to ergonomic and psychosocial hazards while performing deliveries. These findings provide valuable information for future research on OSH issues in the P-hailing sector and can inform policy development. However, the study's limitation is its small sample size, with only 10 respondents representing riders and service providers. In conclusion, addressing safety and health concerns in P-hailing is crucial for the well-being of freelance deliverers and the sustainability of the industry.

Keywords: delivery service, rider, P-hailing, occupational safety and health, Malaysia

1. Introduction

The COVID-19 pandemic has monumentally changed the landscape of the global economy, including Malaysia's. Many economic sectors that were previously competitive and experiencing growth, such as the tourism, hotel, automotive, and aerospace industries, experienced a sharp decline in fortunes. On the other hand, the pandemic has caused a spike in demand within the food delivery and goods packaging sectors [1]. The estimated market size for online food delivery worldwide is around 107.44 billion U.S. dollars for 2019 and is projected to be 154.34 billion U.S. dollars by 2023. Meanwhile, Malaysia's online food delivery market has also shown exponential growth of 18.6% from 2017 to 2020 [2]. Based on these facts, this research opined that by the year 2022, the food delivery business will become one of the fastest-growing business sectors worldwide, including in developing countries.

In addition, this maturing development trajectory has resulted in the increased usage of the application of online digital technologies within certain industries for maintaining a business entity's competitiveness in the market [3]. Technological applications that utilize the Internet such as smartphones have changed the way society conducts business and individual daily lifestyles. According to Ghajargar et al. [4], demand for home delivery services is rising due to online shopping as this service is having the coverage of large geographic areas. The consumers enjoy these applications and their delivery services because it brings greatest convenience to their daily lives.

Besides, the enforcement of the Movement Control Order (MCO), Conditional Movement Control Order (CMCO), and Recovery Movement Control Order (RMCO) in Malaysia, during the pandemic, also have given opportunities to the food industry moving their traditional approach business to digital delivery services. There is now a huge variety of companies offering food delivery services *via* digital platforms in Malaysia, including Foodpanda, Lalamove, GrabFood, and Halo Delivery, whereby local motorcycle riders are engaged to deliver food and parcel. According to a newspaper article [5], Foodpanda has 30,000 riders working for them around the country. This scenario greatly stimulated the digital market-based economy (gig economy). Gig economy is the manifestation of a trend toward a free market-based digital e-commerce platform that is characterized by short-term and long-term contracts between organizations and individuals with both permanent occupancies and freelancers. This system is also driven by the digital environment and application readiness that directly lead to the generation of job opportunities [5].

Previous studies [6] explained that the gig economy can be divided mainly into two forms, "crowdwork" and "work-on-demand *via* app." "Crowdwork" refers to employment activities that require the performance of a series of tasks through an online platform, while "work-on-demand *via* app" involves work where the performance of tasks is in a traditional mode, for instance, transportation and cleaning services. Delivery services provided by motorcycle riders are part of this category even though some of them might offer their services personally without a middle platform. They deal directly with their clients or users commonly *via* mobile phones. Once hired and completed the job, the payment will be transferred to the bank account. In short, the concept of digital labor or digital gig workforce is a free-market system where the transactions are task-based and the workers work independently without being bound to long-term contracts with any company [7]. Even though gig economy offers many opportunities to gig workers, such as flexible work environment, working in interest areas, and access to global job postings, freelancers face many challenges in the form of less payment, lack of social benefit, and job security [8].

The rapid increase in the number of permanent workers and freelancers operating in the digital e-commerce platform sector has created a need for a more efficient method of management, especially in terms of occupational safety and health (OSH). The freelance deliverers face numerous safety and health hazards when performing deliveries as they are mostly working outdoors, specifically on the road. Based on past studies, food and parcel delivery riders reported experiencing occupational stress, health risk, and burnout [9, 10] that were positively associated with the number of motor vehicle accidents [11].

Therefore, this study is focusing on determining safety and health issues among food and parcel delivery riders in Malaysia. In specific, present study determined what are the occupational safety as well as health hazards faced by the P-hailing riders in Malaysia. The findings of this research should fill the gap in the literature pertaining to OSH in P-hailing sectors that is limited to found worldwide or in

Malaysia. Moreover, the research result is expected to serve as an initial reference for the government or policymaker to construct an appropriate OSH management and compliance system for P-hailing sector.

Overall, this research explored issues pertaining to OSH among P-hailing freelance riders registered with parcel and food delivery service providers using digital platforms (i.e., Grab, Foodpanda, Lalamove, and Ninja Delivery) in Malaysia. Besides conducting reviews on related literature, several interview sessions were conducted with the riders from all states of Malaysia, as well as executives representing the P-hailing companies to determine the issues. Finally, occupational safety and health hazards related to P-hailing were distinguished and suggestions were proposed for better OSH management and compliance in this sector.

2. Occupational safety and health (OSH) issues in the P-hailing sector

In this study, P-hailing (*parcel hailing*) refers to the sector that provides services for food/drinks and parcels using digital platforms, through their registered freelance motorists [12–14]. Therefore, this research is limited to OSH issues involving the P-hailing deliverers in Malaysia. In fact, it is very difficult to obtain statistical data relating to occupational accidents in this sector. However, motor vehicle accidents involving P-hailing riders are frequently reported by media and attract the attention of society. A recent study [15] found that P-hailing workers endure 30 dangerous situations and five near misses every hour in a typical day of work, thus exacerbating the need for research toward OSH management and compliance within this sector at the earliest. This section provides further explanation of OSH issues in the P-hailing sector, covering road accidents and other occupational hazards that exist in the industry.

2.1 Road accidents

Road accidents remain a pressing issue in Malaysia, especially affecting those who use motorcycles. This includes the food and parcel deliverers who have to perform their tasks under intense time constraints to fulfill customer demands, which then indirectly lead them to commit risky riding or driving behaviors [16]. Recently, a sharp increase has been observed in the total number of P-hailing deliverers because of the development of e-commerce. Online business has received intense coverage in Malaysia because of breakthroughs in the development of technology, which help to speed up the purchasing process compared to the traditional method employed physically. In addition, the COVID-19 pandemic has served as a catalyst for the drastic rise in the number of P-hailing deliverers.

Basically, P-hailing deliverers prefer using motorcycles for several reasons. These factors include better mobility, low cost, and the ability to perform faster deliveries, which is crucial for those engaged with digital food and beverage delivery providers such as Foodpanda, GrabFood, Bungkus It, and other platforms [17]. It is also found that the deliverers have to complete numerous delivery tasks within a limited period of time to satisfy the customers [18]. Therefore, the primary issue in the P-hailing sector concerns vehicular accidents due to the nature of P-hailing work requiring the usage of motorcycles that leave riders at a high risk of road accidents while performing their duties. This is proven by a statistic reported by Lee [19], whereby two thirds (more than 1700) of the 2576 fatal motorcycle accident cases throughout the Movement Control Order (MCO) period involved P-hailing delivery riders. Accidents involving deliverers are rooted in dangerous driving and violations of traffic lights, which are committed by deliverers in the name of completing deliveries on time.

Datuk Seri Wee Ka Siong, the (then) Minister of Transportation, remarked that young P-hailing riders are the group most involved in fatal accidents, with an estimated 12 accidents occurring on a daily basis [20]. The fact that P-hailing riders are considered as essential service workers paints a grim picture of the total number of accidents occurring. In addition, the Ministry of Transportation also reported an increase of up to 200 new P-hailing riders on a daily basis [20] as a result of mass lay-offs and the resulting lack of income for these new riders as a result of the MCO. The Ministry of Human Resources also released a report which revealed that nearly 100,000 employees had been laid off since the previous October [20], which results in pressure within Malaysian society due to the continued enforcement of the MCO. The statistics of accidents in the P-hailing sector are compared with similar statistics from the traditional delivery sector, as showcased in **Figures 1–3**.

P-hailing, therefore, provides an opportunity for many people to sustain their livelihood. The fact that most of these riders are the breadwinners of their families adds to the sense of urgency for tackling this issue, according to the Royal Malaysian Police (PDRM) [20]. A factor contributing to deliverers' reckless behavior on the road is the system used by providers that incentivize timeliness of deliveries. Failure to finish deliveries on time results in customers giving deliverers a low rating, thus affecting their payment. Based on research data obtained from the Malaysian Institute of Road Safety Research (MIROS), 70% of deliverers show reckless behavior during peak hours such as increasing the motorcycle speed limits to complete the delivery process. The deliverers were also under strict time limits to complete their deliveries, with failure resulting in a demotion of their rating, which directly affects their employment fees. Thus, these factors have contributed to deliverers violating traffic rules in the name of completing their deliveries as soon as possible. This pressure of time involved in just-in-time work has significant implications for road safety [21]. Other studies also stated that during lockdowns, delivery on demand rises making riders tend to speed, and generally, the risk of serious or even fatal crashes increases with higher vehicular speeds [22, 23].

Based on the observations of the Malaysian Institute of Road Safety Research (MIROS), 70% of P-hailing deliverers exhibit behaviors that leave them at risk of accidents especially during the peak hours of 11 a.m. to 2 p.m., such as parking in yellow squares, riding through red lights, and using phones while riding [19]. Prior work has highlighted that 55.3% of fast-food delivery workers in Malaysia use nonstandard helmets. Besides, a conducted study [24] on work-related factors underlying risky driving behavior of food delivery riders in Athens found that the young food delivery

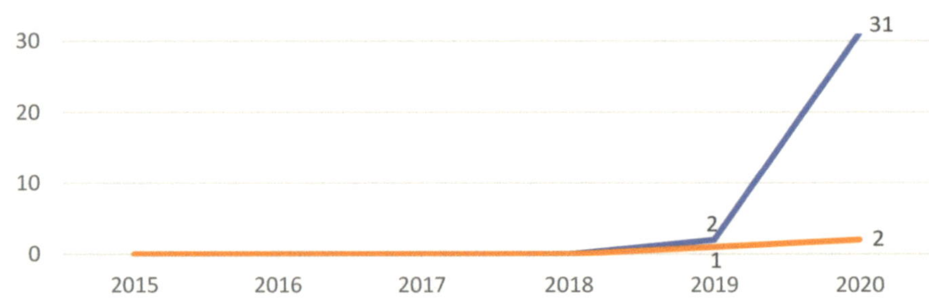

Figure 1.
Statistics of fatal accidents involving deliverers (2015–20).

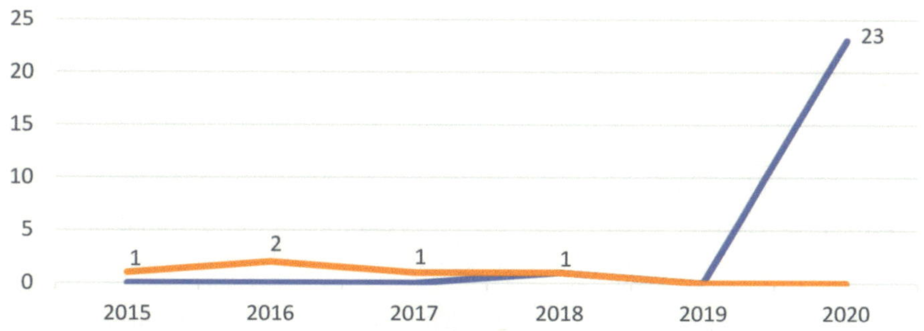

Figure 2.
Statistics of severe injuries sustained by deliverers (2015–20).

Figure 3.
Statistics of accidents resulting in light injuries for deliverers (2015–20).

riders are more likely to participate in dangerous riding behaviors that involve critical traffic offenses like "red-light running" and "helmet nonuse," which appear to relate to various stresses or motives for the riders. Therefore, it is crystal clear that the issue involving the road safety of P-hailing deliverers is a significant one. Deliverers are advised not to be too focused on performing their deliveries on time to the extent of exhibiting dangerous behavior on the road.

2.2 Occupational safety and health (OSH) hazards in the P-hailing sector

The digital food delivery services sector involves orders received, packaging, and delivery to customers. The gig courier or rider job requires few skills and is easily obtained but they are precarious, physically demanding, and mentally stressful, especially for motorcycle and e-bicycle riders, who are more exposed to hazards. Therefore, besides addressing the road-accident issues, this research also determined other related OSH hazards faced by the P-hailing riders. According to a report released by the International Labour Organization (ILO) (2000) and another study by Lee [19], these are the OSH hazards associated with the P-hailing sector:

a. Smoke from other vehicles

b. Direct exposure to UV rays (from the sunlight)

c. Extreme environment/climate temperatures (i.e., heat/cold stress)

d. Vibrations

e. Biological hazards (i.e., virus andbacteria)

f. Ergonomic hazards (i.e., prolonged sitting and awkward postures)

g. Psychosocial hazards (e.g., stress, customer complaints, and sexual harassment)

Research [19] explained in detail that deliverers need to carry the ordered items throughout their delivery journey, which can be extremely long, potentially leading to work stress, and exhaustion due to a lack of rest. In addition, food and beverage deliverers often find themselves facing the same situation with lack of rest due to their working time requirements [21].

Besides those references, Ibrahim et al. [15] outlined the hazards that carry a risk of accidents among the delivery riders. The hazards are as follows:

a. Objects obstructing the road

b. Defected road surfaces

c. Construction works and the existence of walking/cycling paths

d. Limited driver/rider vision

3. Ambiguity of employment status

The ambiguity of nature deliverers' employment status poses a problem to the agencies in charge of OSH enforcement and management, such as DOSH in enforcing OSH laws on all P-hailing service-providing companies. This situation also leads provider companies to not emphasize OSH management for their freelance deliverers, with their stand being that the deliverers are not their employees. Thus, the unclear status of the freelance contracts between deliverers and providers has also contributed to a low enforcement of OSH policies, with providers stating that since deliverers themselves are vendors, they are responsible for their own safety, health, and welfare. As per stipulated in the Occupational Safety and Health Act 1994, a self-employed need to secure their own safety and health while performing his/her job or tasks [25].

Since gig riders are part of an informal economy like other gig workers, they may lack access to paid or sick leave, social protection, and income protection like other employers even though they are registered with P-hailing service providers.

4. The importance of addressing safety and health issues in the P-hailing sector

Occupational health and safety are concerned with ensuring and providing a safe environment for all employees at a workplace. Research pertaining to occupational safety and health provides valuable input to the government in laying down the required focus and priorities for carrying out enforcement activities, developing and promoting a standard to employers in certain sectors to reduce the rate of accidents. The compliance with OSH-related legislations also enables to contribute the sustainability of the industry's competitiveness by optimizing safe and healthy manpower besides decent working environment.

Based on past studies, food and parcel delivery riders reported experiencing several OSH issues namely occupational stress, health risk, and burnout [9, 11, 26] that were positively associated with the number of motor vehicle accidents. As food and parcel delivery nowadays experience a massive demand that contributes to the profit growth of the delivery business, it is important for the stakeholders to seriously address OSH issues within the sectors.

5. Discussion

Based on the responses of the 15 interviewed deliverers, the nature of their jobs leads them to commit risky riding as well as cutting corners, including violating road-traffic rules. The violations of rules are including jumping a red traffic light, making a U-turn inappropriately, overspeeding, and not properly wearing shoes while making deliveries. Moreover, riders from the city areas such as Kuala Lumpur, Johor Bahru, and Penang admitted that without violating such rules, they are unable to complete the orders within the demanded time.

On the other hand, the deliverers who use motorcycles to conduct tasks need to work long hours or ride long distances to earn more income. Thus, they revealed that they are suffering from musculoskeletal disorders such as back and neck pain. The riders also stated that delivering parcels or food also exposed them to the risk of COVID-19.

To summarize the findings, food and parcel delivery drivers using motorcycles face a range of occupational safety and health hazards, namely exposure to bad weather conditions (i.e., heavy rain, extremely hot weather, and thunderstorms), exposure to air pollution from other vehicles' emissions, and the risk of being hit by cars, trucks, and other vehicles on the road. Moreover, the P-Hailing riders are also threatened by ergonomic hazards such as physical strain from carrying heavy loads. In addition, they may experience fatigue and stress from working long hours and meeting tight delivery deadlines.

To be specific, present research findings revealed that food/parcel delivery riders in Malaysia face a variety of occupational health hazards, including:

i. Ergonomics hazards: Riders are at risk of musculoskeletal injuries from repetitive motions, such as prolonged sitting on a motorcycle or bicycle, as well as injuries from traffic accidents.

ii. Environmental hazards: Riders are exposed to the elements, such as extreme heat or cold, and may also be exposed to air pollution from traffic.

iii. Psychological hazards: Riders may face stress from time pressures and traffic hazards, as well as social isolation.

iv. Health hazards: Riders may be at risk of respiratory issues due to prolonged exposure to traffic pollution, as well as heart disease and stroke due to sedentary lifestyle.

Moreover, the food/parcel delivery riders who are engaged with P-hailing service providers also face various occupational safety hazards, including road-traffic accident hazards. The hazards are such as:

i. Traffic accidents: Delivery riders are at a high risk of being involved in traffic accidents due to the nature of their work, which requires them to travel on roads and highways.

ii. Weather hazards: Delivery riders may be exposed to extreme weather conditions, such as rain, snow, and heat, which can lead to injuries and illnesses.

iii. Slip, trip, and fall hazards: Delivery riders may be at risk of slips, trips, and falls while delivering food, particularly when navigating uneven or poorly lit surfaces.

iv. Aggression and violence: Delivery riders may be at risk of aggression and violence from customers or members of the public.

In Malaysia, the Department of Occupational Safety and Health (DOSH) released a guideline for the Occupational Safety and Health Act 1994 that must be enforced by all employers and employees in Malaysia to ensure that a safe working culture is practiced in conjunction with a safe working environment. The responsibility for ensuring safety is held by both employers and employees, with the latter needing to understand their underlying responsibilities such as adhering to safety measures as prescribed by the law, following safety and health procedures released by the company's management as well as wearing appropriate riding apparels, including personal protection equipment (PPE).

Based on present research, to improve the health and safety of food/parcel delivery riders, expanding the knowledge/awareness in terms of occupational safety and health hazards and their responsibilities to ensure their workplace safety (as well as health) is crucial. Safety training enables employees to gain knowledge related to work-related hazards and the associated risks [27–29].

Thus, occupational safety and health (OSH) issues can have a significant impact on the sustainability of a business in the food/parcel delivery industry. If the deliverers are not properly protected from all the explained hazards, it can lead to injuries and illnesses, resulting in lost productivity.

6. Conclusion

In conclusion, growth in demand for the food and parcel delivery sectors in Malaysia within these few years increased the number of riders. As discussed above, the riders face work-related safety and health issues like road accidents and exposed hazard issues during completion of the delivery process.

The practice of adherence to occupational safety and health procedures is crucial for the long-term sustainability of the digital food/goods delivery sector. Therefore, the government has remarked on the requirement of a new mechanism to tackle issues involving the safety, health, and welfare of these workers. The creation of specific guidelines is important for empowering workers and cultivating a culture of maintaining their occupational safety and health. This will ensure the sustainability of the P-hailing business in Malaysia.

OSH (occupational safety and health) management is important for the food/parcel delivery sectors in terms of business sustainability for several reasons, which are as follows:

i. Compliance with legal regulations: OSH management ensures that delivery riders are in compliance with all relevant laws and regulations related to safety and health at work. This helps to prevent fines and legal penalties that can be costly for them as self-employed workers.

ii. Reduced accidents and injuries: OSH management can help to reduce the number of accidents and injuries among the P-hailing delivery riders, which can disturb their productivity and quality of services.

iii. Improved employee morale: When employees feel safe and healthy at work, they are more likely to be satisfied with their job and have a positive attitude toward their employers. This can lead to increased employee retention and lower turnover rates.

iv. Positive reputation: A business that prioritizes OSH management is likely to be viewed positively by customers, regulators, and the general public. This can help to build a positive reputation and attract new customers.

v. Increased productivity: The P-hailing delivery riders who feel that their safety and health at work are monitored by the engaging companies as well as the government, will more likely to be productive and efficient, which can help to improve the bottom line for the overall business.

Occupational safety and health (OSH) issues can have a significant impact on the sustainability of a business in the food delivery industry. If employees are not properly trained and protected from hazards, it can lead to injuries and illnesses, resulting in lost productivity, increased healthcare costs, and possible legal action. This can also lead to a decrease in employee morale and turnover, which can further impact the business's ability to maintain operations and customer satisfaction. Additionally, if a company has a reputation for poor OSH practices, it can damage the company's reputation and lead to decreased consumer trust and a decline in sales. Therefore, it is important for food delivery businesses to prioritize and invest in OSH programs to ensure the safety and well-being of their employees, while also protecting the sustainability of their business.

7. Limitation of the study

The study was conducted among 15 food/parcel delivery riders, thus sample size was small, which may not be representative of the larger population, as well as bound to a limited generalisability. Moreover, even though the interview was conducted in various locations in Peninsula Malaysia, the results may not be generalizable to other regions.

In addition, the study findings solely relied on the interview answers, which may be subject to bias.

For future research suggestions, it is recommended that a cross-sectional, quantitative study involving a larger sample size could be used to increase the generalizability of the findings. Furthermore, the study could be replicated in multiple locations to examine regional differences, especially among the samples in Borneo region.

Using objective measures, such as physiological data obtained by using survey questions, is also proposed to reduce bias in the data.

8. Contributions of the study

This study supported the academia by offering initial references on OSH issues pertaining to the P-hailing sector. In specific, theoretical implications include a better understanding of the specific risks and hazards faced by the P-hailing delivery riders, as well as the factors that contribute to those risks. This knowledge can then be used to inform the development of interventions and policies aimed at reducing those risks and improving the overall safety and health of the sector.

Managerial implications include the need for the P-hailing companies to take a proactive approach to identifying and addressing the risks and hazards faced by their deliverers. This may involve implementing policies and procedures to protect riders, such as providing training and education on safe riding practices and providing personal protective equipment. It may also involve implementing technology solutions to improve rider safety, such as GPS tracking and communication systems.

Moreover, it also implies that P-hailing business providers should also conduct regular safety assessments, in order to identify and mitigate potential hazards and to ensure that riders are adequately protected and provided with safe working conditions. Additionally, it may be necessary to work with other organizations and stakeholders, such as government agencies and labor unions, to create a safe working environment for food/parcel delivery riders.

Author details

Syazwan Syah Zulkifly
School of Business Management, Universiti Utara Malaysia, Sintok, Kedah, Malaysia

*Address all correspondence to: syazwan.syah@uum.edu.my

References

[1] Ramli N, Abd Ghani F, Nawawi WNW, Abd Majid HAM. Intention to use online food ordering services among universities students during COVID-19 pandemic. International Journal of Academic Research in Business & Social Sciences. 2021;**11**(13):394-405. DOI: 10.6007/ijarbss/v11-i13/8556

[2] Hooi R, Leong TK, Yee LH. "Intention to use online food delivery service in Malaysia among university students," in Conference on Management, Business, Innovation, Education and Social Science. 2021;**1**(1):60-73 [Online]. Available: https://journal.uib.ac.id/index.php/combines/article/view/4415

[3] Whitelaw S, Mamas MA, Topol E, Van Spall HGC. Applications of digital technology in COVID-19 pandemic planning and response. The Lancet Digital Health. 2020;**2**(8):e435-e440. DOI: 10.1016/S2589-7500(20)30142-4

[4] Ghajargar M, Zenezini G, Montanaro T. Home delivery services: Innovations and emerging needs. IFAC-Papers OnLine. 2016;**49**(12):1371-1376. DOI: 10.1016/j.ifacol.2016.07.755

[5] Lizawati B. Ekonomi gig: Alternatif kekalkan perniagaan, persediaan hadapi pasca COVID 19. Kuala Lumpur: Bernama; 2020

[6] De Stefano VM. Introduction: Crowdsourcing, the gig-economy, and the law. Comparative Labor Law & Policy Journal. 2016;**37**(3):461-470

[7] Rahim AFA, Yaacob NA, Noor RM, Najid NA, Zulkifli N. Strengthening the gig economy: Future of digital labor workforce platform post-Covid-19. GADING Journal of Social and Sciences. 2021;**24**(04):17-26

[8] Roy G, Shrivastava AK. Future of gig economy: Opportunities and challenges. IMI Konnect. 2020;**9**(1):14-25 [Online]. Available: https://imikonnect.imik.edu.in/uploads/issue_file/3590503Mod_imiKonnect_January_March_2020.pdf#page=18

[9] Huang H. Riders on the storm: Amplified platform precarity and the impact of COVID-19 on online food-delivery drivers in China. Journal of Contemporary China. 2022;**31**(135):351-365. DOI: 10.1080/10670564.2021.1966895

[10] Zhang C, Sitar S, Huang CC. Effects of job demands and resources on positive and negative affect of delivery drivers in China. International Journal of Environmental Research and Public Health. 2022;**19**(13):2-11. DOI: 10.3390/ijerph19138140

[11] Alonso F, Esteban C, Gonzalez-Marin A, Alfaro E, Useche SA. Job stress and emotional exhaustion at work in Spanish workers: Does unhealthy work affect the decision to drive? PLoS One. 2020;**15**(1):1-17. DOI: 10.1371/journal.pone.0227328

[12] Loke SF. Pemberitahuan Pertanyaan Dewan Rakyat Mesyuarat Kedua, Penggal Ketiga Parlimen ke-14. 2020

[13] Morshed SA, Khan SS, Tanvir RB, Nur S. Impact of COVID-19 pandemic on ride-hailing services based on large-scale twitter data analysis. Journal of Urban Management. 2021;**10**(2):155-165. DOI: 10.1016/j.jum.2021.03.002

[14] Ravindran S. Subsidy for 3,000 p-hailing riders. The Star. 2021. Available from: hestar.com.my/metro/metro-news/2021/08/26/subsidy-for-3000-p-hailing-riders#:~:text=The%20

programme%20offers%20youths%20aged,Organisation%20contribution%20for%20a%20year

[15] Ibrahim MKA, Hamzah A, Abu Kassim KA. Measurement of riding situation awareness among Malaysian motorcyclists using a video-based assessment approach. International Journal of Road Safety. 2021;**2**(1):4-9

[16] Convery E et al. Work Health and Safety of Food Delivery Workers in the Gig Economy. Sidney, Australia: Centre for WSH, NSW Government; 2020 [Online]. Available: http://www.centreforwhs.nsw.gov.au/__data/assets/pdf_file/0007/932677/Work-health-and-safety-of-food-delivery-workers-in-the-gig-economy..pdf

[17] Vijayasankari A, Indra S, Kalpana S. Prevalence of road traffic accident among food delivery workers in southern Chennai. IOSR Journal of Nursing Health Science. 2020;**9**(3):17-20. DOI: 10.9790/1959-0903061720

[18] Lu X, Guo X, Zhang J, Li X. Reducing traffic violations in the online food delivery industry — A case study in xi ' an City, China. Public Health. 2022;**10**:1-14. DOI: 10.3389/fpubh.2022.974488

[19] Lee B. Working conditions and health status of delivery workers. Korean Journal of Occupational Health Nursing. 2019;**28**(3):156-165. DOI: 10.5807/kjohn.2019.28.3.156

[20] Bernama. Penunggang p-hailing catat kematian tertinggi 9 bulan PKP tahun lalu. Metro; 2021

[21] Christie N, Ward H. The health and safety risks for people who drive for work in the gig economy. Journal of Transport and Health. 2019;**13**(February):115-127. DOI: 10.1016/j.jth.2019.02.007

[22] Aarts L, Van Schagen I. Driving speed and the risk of road crashes: A review. Accident; Analysis and Prevention. 2006;**38**(2):215-224. DOI: 10.1016/j.aap.2005.07.004

[23] Nguyen ATT et al. Health and safety risks faced by delivery riders during the Covid-19 pandemic. Journal of Transport and Health. 2022;**25**(January):1-12

[24] Papakostopoulos V, Nathanael D. The complex interrelationship of work-related factors underlying risky driving behavior of food delivery riders in Athens, Greece. Safety and Health at Work. 2021;**12**(2):147-153. DOI: 10.1016/j.shaw.2020.10.006

[25] DOSH. Occupational Safety and Health Act 1994. Malaysia: Department of Occupational Safety and Health; 1994. p.31. Available from: www.dosh.gov.my

[26] Ye X, Ren S, Li X, Wang Z. The mediating role of psychological capital between perceived management commitment and safety behavior. Journal of Safety Research. 2020;**72**(December):29-40. DOI: 10.1016/j.jsr.2019.12.004

[27] Vinodkumar MN, Bhasi M. Safety management practices and safety behaviour: Assessing the mediating role of safety knowledge and motivation. Accident; Analysis and Prevention. 2010;**42**(2010):2082-2093. DOI: 10.1016/j.aap.2010.06.021

[28] Khoo TH, Surienty L, Selamat MN. Safety training and safety behaviour in the malaysian SME. Journal of Occupational Safety and Health. 2016;**13**(2):55-62

[29] Ajmal M, Isha ASN, Nordin SM, Al-Mekhlafi ABA. Safety-management practices and the occurrence of occupational accidents: Assessing the mediating role of safety compliance. Sustainability. 2022;**14**(8):2-17. DOI: 10.3390/su14084569